The Depression

Understanding, Facing, and Overcoming Inner Darkness

Author: Ojeda

ISBN: 9798343168037

Publisher: Independently published

DEDICATION

Contenido

Prologue

Depression is one of the most common yet misunderstood illnesses of our time. Despite advances in research and greater access to information, a cloud of stigma and misconceptions still surrounds this condition that affects millions of people worldwide. As a doctor, I have witnessed firsthand the silent suffering of many individuals who, trapped in their darkness, struggle to find a way out. This is one of the reasons why this book is so important.

The purpose of these pages is simple yet crucial: to provide an understandable, practical, and evidence-based guide to depression. It is a journey that will allow us to understand what this illness truly is, why it affects us, and, most importantly, what we can do to overcome it. In my practice, I have treated people who, despite their pain, were afraid to speak about it for fear of being judged, dismissed, or ignored. In a society that often values productivity or the appearance of happiness above all else, feeling overwhelmed is often seen as a sign of weakness or personal failure.

But depression is neither a weakness nor a failure. It is an illness, and as such, it deserves to be treated with the same respect and attention as any other physical ailment. It is not a matter of willpower or simply "thinking positively." Those who suffer from depression do not choose to be in that state, just as no one chooses to have a heart attack or a broken bone.

In this book, I aim to explain in simple terms the mechanisms behind depression from both a medical and psychological perspective. This is not about miracle cures or empty promises; rather, it is about offering real, proven tools that can help those suffering from this illness, as well as their family members and friends, to better understand and cope with it.

Furthermore, this journey will not be solely theoretical. Throughout the chapters, you will find practical examples, real-life cases, and exercises that I have seen work for people just like you. Sometimes, the first battle is acknowledging that there is a problem, and the second is having the courage to ask for help. This book may serve as that first extended hand for those who feel lost.

The challenge of depression is immense, but it is not insurmountable. My hope is that, by the time you finish reading this book, you will feel that there is a path toward the light—a path that, although difficult, can be taken step by step, with the right support and the necessary knowledge. Because depression, though powerful, does not define the person who suffers from it.

This book is for you, for those who suffer in silence, and for those who love and care for someone who does. It is an invitation to open your eyes, heart, and mind to a deeper and more compassionate understanding of depression and to work together toward healing.

Welcome.

Introduction: What Depression Is and How It Affects Our Lives

Discussing depression involves delving into a complex topic that has been the subject of scientific studies for decades, yet it remains a source of misunderstanding for many. This deep distress, affecting both mind and body, not only impacts the individual suffering from it but also their loved ones, work environment, and overall health. Understanding depression is an essential first step toward addressing it effectively and without prejudice.

1.1. Scientific Definition of Depression

Depression is a mental disorder characterized by a persistently low mood, accompanied by a loss of interest or pleasure in daily activities, feelings of hopelessness, and a lack of energy that can last for weeks, months, or even years. Unlike occasional sadness, which is a normal response to life's difficulties, depression is a medical condition that significantly disrupts an individual's daily life.

According to the American Psychiatric Association (APA), depression, also known as major depressive disorder, involves a series of emotional, physical, and cognitive symptoms that must be present for at least two consecutive weeks to be clinically diagnosed. These symptoms include, but are not limited to, profound sadness, loss of interest in activities once enjoyed, changes in appetite or sleep patterns, fatigue, feelings of worthlessness or guilt, and recurrent thoughts of death or suicide.

Depression is not simply "feeling sad" or "going through a rough patch." It is a real illness, with biological, psychological, and social roots. Understanding this is crucial to properly addressing both its diagnosis and treatment.

1.2. Types of Depression: Major, Dysthymia, Seasonal, and More

Not all forms of depression are the same. There are different types, each with its own characteristics, and it's important to know them in order to correctly identify symptoms and seek appropriate treatment.

- **Major Depression**: This is the most well-known form of depression and the one most commonly associated with the term. It is characterized by intense episodes that can last for weeks or months, marked by deep sadness, hopelessness, and lack of energy. People with major depression may feel incapable of performing even the simplest tasks, such as getting out of bed or holding everyday conversations.

- **Dysthymia or Persistent Depressive Disorder**: Unlike major depression, dysthymia is a milder disorder but lasts much longer, often for years. People suffering from dysthymia live in a constant state of sadness or apathy, but without episodes as severe as those in major depression. Often, this form of depression goes unnoticed because the symptoms are less intense, but its prolonged duration can have a profound impact on quality of life.

- **Seasonal Affective Disorder (SAD)**: This type of depression is related to seasonal changes and is more common during the winter months when sunlight is scarcer. People with SAD experience the same symptoms of depression, but in a cycle that follows the seasons. During the winter months, they may feel fatigued, sad, and low on energy, while these symptoms tend to disappear in spring or summer.

- **Postpartum Depression**: After childbirth, some women experience a specific form of depression linked to hormonal changes and the emotional and physical responsibilities of caring for a baby. This depression can appear in the weeks or months following the child's birth and is characterized by feelings of sadness, extreme exhaustion, anxiety, and difficulty bonding emotionally with the baby.

- **Atypical Depression**: Unlike classic depression, people with atypical depression experience temporary improvements in mood when positive events occur, but they quickly return to a depressive state. Additionally, symptoms can include increased sensitivity to rejection and a sensation of heaviness in the limbs.

1.3. How to Recognize the Symptoms of Depression

Recognizing depression is not always easy. Many people live with it in silence, hiding their distress due to fear of social judgment or misunderstanding. However, there are clear signs that can alert us to its presence:

- **Mood Changes**: Persistent sadness, unexplained crying, irritability, or constant anxiety are indicators that something is not right.

- **Loss of Interest**: When activities that used to bring pleasure, such as hobbies, sports, or spending time with friends, no longer seem interesting, it may be a symptom of depression.

- **Fatigue and Lack of Energy**: Depression can make even the simplest tasks seem impossible. People with depression often feel exhausted all the time, even after resting.

- **Changes in Appetite and Sleep**: Some people with depression lose their appetite completely, while others may overeat as a way to fill an emotional void. Similarly, some experience insomnia, while others sleep excessively.

- **Difficulty Concentrating**: A person's mind may feel clouded, making it hard to make decisions or focus on simple tasks.

- **Suicidal Thoughts or Thoughts of Death**: In severe cases, depression can lead to recurrent thoughts of death or suicide. These thoughts should never be ignored and require immediate medical attention.

1.4. The Impact on Quality of Life: Relationships, Work, and Health

Depression does not only affect an individual internally; it also has repercussions in all aspects of their life. Personal relationships are often severely impacted, as the lack of energy or interest can make communication and maintaining emotional bonds difficult. People with depression may become withdrawn, leading to conflicts with friends, family, or partners who don't understand what is happening.

In the workplace, depression can have a devastating impact. Lack of concentration, absenteeism, and reduced productivity are common consequences. Many individuals with depression struggle to meet their responsibilities, which can lead to job loss or serious career setbacks.

Lastly, physical health is also affected. Depression is associated with a higher incidence of chronic diseases, such as cardiovascular problems, diabetes, and sleep disorders. Moreover, the lack of motivation to take care of oneself can lead to neglecting basic health habits, such as diet or exercise, further worsening both physical and mental health.

In summary, depression comprehensively affects both the individual and their environment. It is not just a problem of "feelings," but a real illness that requires appropriate attention and treatment. Throughout this book, we will explore how to recognize, confront, and ultimately overcome it.

Chapter 1: The Importance of Recognizing Depression

The first step in addressing any illness is recognizing that it exists. In the case of depression, this process can be particularly challenging due to social stigmas, common myths, and the difficulty in distinguishing it from other emotions like sadness. This chapter focuses on demystifying what depression truly is, identifying its early signs, and understanding the difference between a fleeting emotion and a clinical disorder. Additionally, we will present the case of Juan, an executive who, despite having a life that seemed perfect, was trapped in the darkness of depression.

2.1. Myths and Realities About Depression

There are many myths surrounding depression—erroneous beliefs that complicate its understanding and treatment. Some of these myths perpetuate the idea that depression is simply a lack of willpower or that it can be overcome by "thinking positively." Below, we address some of the most common myths and the reality behind them:

- **Myth 1: Depression is just being sad.**
  The reality is that depression goes far beyond sadness. While sadness is a natural emotion that arises in response to life

events, depression is a mental disorder that involves much deeper symptoms, such as lack of energy, constant hopelessness, and a loss of interest in daily activities.

- **Myth 2: Depression is a sign of weakness.**
  This is one of the most damaging myths. Depression is not a matter of strength or weakness, but an illness that can affect anyone, regardless of their ability to face challenges. Believing it is a sign of weakness only adds to the shame and silence of those suffering from it.

- **Myth 3: If you try hard enough, you can overcome depression.**
  Many people believe that depression can be overcome simply by "thinking positively" or "putting in the effort." However, depression is not something one chooses, nor does it go away through sheer willpower. It is a real illness that requires treatment, whether through therapy, medication, or lifestyle changes.

- **Myth 4: It only affects people who have experienced severe trauma.**
  While traumatic experiences can trigger depression, they are not the only cause. Biological, genetic, environmental, and psychological factors can all contribute to the development of depression, even in people who have not experienced traumatic events.

- **Myth 5: Antidepressants change your personality or make you addicted.**
  Antidepressants are a therapeutic tool that helps regulate chemical imbalances in the brain. They do not change a person's personality nor create addiction, though they can

have side effects that must be monitored by a professional doctor.

2.2. Early Signs Not to Ignore

Depression often sets in gradually. It can start with small changes in mood or energy levels, which are frequently overlooked. Recognizing these early signs is crucial to seeking help before the symptoms worsen. Here are some early indications not to ignore:

- **Unexplained fatigue and lack of energy:** Even after a good night's rest, you feel exhausted at the start of the day. This exhaustion is not related to physical exertion but to a mental state that drains emotional energy.

- **Loss of interest:** Activities you once enjoyed, like going out with friends, playing sports, or even reading, no longer motivate you. You start turning down plans and preferring isolation.

- **Changes in appetite or sleep:** You may notice a loss of appetite or, conversely, feel constantly hungry. The same applies to sleep: you might experience insomnia or sleep excessively, without feeling truly rested.

- **Difficulty concentrating:** Tasks that were once easy become complicated. You struggle to focus at work or in conversations, and your mind constantly wanders.

- **Feelings of worthlessness or guilt:** For no apparent reason, you start feeling worthless or have a deep sense of guilt, even over insignificant matters. These thoughts can become recurrent and intense.

- **Thoughts of death or suicide:** This is one of the most serious signs of depression. If you start thinking that life is not worth living or have thoughts about harming yourself, it is crucial to seek help immediately.

2.3. The Difference Between Sadness and Clinical Depression

It's important to note that feeling sad from time to time is part of the human experience. Sadness can be triggered by events like the loss of a loved one, a breakup, or personal disappointment, and it is usually temporary. Clinical depression, on the other hand, is a prolonged condition that persists even when there is no apparent cause.

- **Duration and persistence:**
  While sadness generally fades with time or as the situation improves, depression lingers for weeks, months, or even years. A depressed person may feel hopeless even in circumstances that would normally bring joy.

- **Impact on functionality:**
  Sadness, though painful, rarely impairs a person's ability to function day-to-day. In contrast, clinical depression can incapacitate a person, making it difficult to get out of bed, go to work, or maintain social relationships.

- **Symptomatology:**
  Sadness is primarily an emotional state, while clinical depression involves physical and cognitive symptoms, such as extreme fatigue, difficulty concentrating, and significant changes in appetite and sleep patterns.

2.4. Case Study: Juan, the Executive Who Had Everything Except Happiness

Juan was a successful man. At 40, he had a thriving career as an executive in a multinational company, a loving family, and a home many dreamed of living in. To others, he seemed to have it all: a respected job, financial stability, and a solid support network. However, Juan felt empty.

Despite fulfilling his daily responsibilities, he experienced a constant fatigue that followed him everywhere. He no longer found joy in his work achievements, and his relationship with his family grew increasingly distant. Each day, upon returning home, he felt unable to share his concerns, and gradually, he began to withdraw. No one noticed that something was wrong; after all, Juan still attended meetings, smiled at social events, and appeared to be doing just fine.

But internally, things were very different. The lack of energy and disinterest in his hobbies, which had once made him happy, led him to distance himself from his friends and stop participating in activities he once enjoyed. He often found himself thinking that his life had no meaning, and although he never seriously considered suicide, the feelings of hopelessness became more frequent.

Finally, after months of denial, Juan decided to see a doctor. After a series of questions, the diagnosis was clear: major depression. Despite his professional success and a family that loved him, depression does not discriminate. With the right support, including therapy and medication, Juan began his path to recovery, learning that depression is not a matter of willpower, but an illness that can affect anyone.

This case illustrates a common reality: depression can hide behind a façade of success and normality. Recognizing the symptoms and seeking help is the first step in overcoming this illness, and understanding that even those who seem to have it all may be struggling with invisible pain is essential to eliminating the stigma surrounding it.

Chapter 2: The Biology of Depression

Depression, though it has psychological and social components, also has a biological foundation that cannot be ignored. Our brain, like any other organ, can experience alterations that affect its functioning, which results in the symptoms of depression. In this chapter, we will explore how brain chemistry, genetics, and neurotransmitters play a crucial role in the onset of this disorder, and how we can support both body and mind through habits that promote the balance of these substances.

3.1. The Depressed Brain: How Brain Chemistry Is Affected

The brain is a complex organ that regulates our emotions, thoughts, and behaviors. In people with depression, certain areas of the brain function differently compared to those without the disorder. One of the main areas affected is the limbic system, which includes structures like the amygdala and hippocampus, responsible for regulating emotions, mood, and memory.

In a depressed brain, studies have shown that there is an imbalance in neuronal activity. The connections between neurons, called synapses, do not function normally, which affects communication between different areas of the brain. This malfunction is often linked to abnormal levels of neurotransmitters, the chemical substances that transmit signals between neurons.

Additionally, MRI scans have shown that some brain areas may shrink in size in people with prolonged depression, especially the hippocampus, which may contribute to the memory loss and difficulty concentrating that many patients experience.

3.2. Genetics and Predisposition: Is Depression Hereditary?

Genetics play an important role in depression, though they do not entirely determine who will develop the disorder. Studies have shown that if one parent suffers from depression, the chances of their child also experiencing it increase significantly. However, genetics alone are not enough to cause depression.

What actually happens is an interaction between genetic and environmental factors. A person may have a genetic predisposition to develop depression, but this does not mean they will necessarily suffer from it. Factors such as stress, emotional trauma, or even physical illnesses can "activate" this predisposition.

One of the most studied genes related to depression is the one that encodes the serotonin transporter protein. Variations in this gene can affect how the brain uses serotonin, which may increase the risk of developing the disorder. However, depression is a complex illness, and while genetics can increase the risk, environmental factors and lifestyle also play a crucial role.

3.3. Hormones and Neurotransmitters: The Role of Serotonin and Dopamine

Neurotransmitters are chemical substances that allow neurons to communicate with each other. In depression, two of the most important neurotransmitters are serotonin and dopamine, though others like norepinephrine are also involved.

- **Serotonin:** Known as the "happiness neurotransmitter," it regulates mood, sleep, appetite, and emotions. In people with depression, serotonin levels in the brain are often reduced, contributing to feelings of sadness, hopelessness, and irritability.

- **Dopamine:** This neurotransmitter is linked to the reward and motivation system. When dopamine levels are low, a person may feel a lack of pleasure in activities they would normally enjoy, known as anhedonia, one of the key symptoms of depression.

- **Norepinephrine:** Though less studied than serotonin and dopamine, norepinephrine is also involved in the stress response and mood regulation. A deficit of this substance may contribute to the fatigue and lack of energy characteristic of depression.

Antidepressants, such as selective serotonin reuptake inhibitors (SSRIs), work by increasing serotonin levels in the brain, allowing neurons to communicate more effectively. Other medications may focus on dopamine or norepinephrine, depending on the specific symptoms of the patient.

3.4. Practical Exercise: How to Foster Habits That Regulate Our Neurotransmitters

While medications are an important tool in treating depression, there are healthy habits that can naturally contribute to the regulation of neurotransmitters in the brain. Below, we propose some practical exercises to foster a healthy chemical balance:

- **Regular Physical Exercise:** Physical activity, especially aerobic exercise like walking, running, or swimming, increases serotonin and dopamine levels. Try to do at least 30 minutes of moderate exercise five times a week. If starting is difficult, set small goals, like walking for 10 minutes a day, and gradually increase the time.

- **Balanced Diet:** Certain foods can positively influence neurotransmitter production. Tryptophan, an amino acid found in foods like turkey, chicken, bananas, and nuts, is essential for serotonin production. Likewise, foods rich in omega-3, such as oily fish, can improve brain function and help combat depression.

- **Good Sleep:** Sleep is essential for neurotransmitter balance. Lack of sleep directly affects serotonin levels, which can worsen depression symptoms. Try to establish a regular sleep routine and avoid using electronic devices at least one hour before bed.

- **Relaxation and Meditation Practices:** Techniques like mindfulness meditation or deep breathing help reduce cortisol levels (the stress hormone) and promote a state of relaxation that supports chemical balance in the brain. Dedicate 10 minutes a day to breathing exercises or meditation to improve your emotional well-being.

- **Exposure to Sunlight:** Exposure to natural light helps regulate serotonin and melatonin levels, substances that influence mood and sleep. If possible, take a walk outside during the day, especially in the early morning. If you live in an area with little sunlight, consider using light therapy lamps to compensate for the lack of exposure.

- **Social Connections:** Maintaining positive social relationships can also stimulate neurotransmitter production. Although depression often leads to a desire to isolate, making the effort to stay in touch with friends and family can improve mood. Even a brief conversation with a loved one can be enough to boost dopamine and serotonin levels.

Healthy Habits Log:

To implement these changes, we suggest creating a weekly habits log. In it, you can write down your daily goals related to exercise, diet, sleep, and social activities. Each day, evaluate how you feel physically and mentally, and if you notice any positive changes in your mood.

For example:

Day	Exercise (minutes)	Balanced Diet	Sleep (hours)	Meditation (minutes)	Social Contact	**Mood (1-10)**
Monday	30	Yes	7	10	Call with friend	6
Tuesday	20	No	6	5	None	4
Wednesday	40	Yes	8	15	Lunch with coworker	7

The goal of this log is to help you identify which habits have a positive impact on your mood and which may need adjustments. Over time, you will be able to adjust your daily activities to promote greater chemical balance in your brain.

This chapter has shown how the biology of depression involves genetic, hormonal, and neurotransmitter factors, but also how we can influence these processes through healthy habits. The key lies in a comprehensive approach that combines medical treatment with natural strategies that promote physical and mental well-being.

Chapter 3: The Psychological Factors of Depression

In addition to the biological aspects, depression is also deeply influenced by psychological factors. Our thoughts, beliefs, and perceptions about ourselves and the world can fuel and perpetuate the depressive state. In this chapter, we will explore how negative self-talk and learned helplessness contribute to depression and how cognitive-behavioral therapy (CBT) provides powerful tools to change our thinking and transform our emotional state.

4.1. Negative Self-Talk: How Our Thoughts Drag Us Down

One of the most common traits in people with depression is negative self-talk. This term refers to the automatic thoughts that arise in our minds, often critical, pessimistic, or destructive. In depression, these types of thoughts tend to be recurrent and extremely harmful, contributing to a downward spiral of sadness, anxiety, and hopelessness.

Negative self-talk can take many forms. Some examples include:

- "I'm not good enough."

- "Everything I do is wrong."

- "I'll never be happy."

- "Nobody cares about me."

These thoughts are often irrational, but they are so persistent that people start to believe them as absolute truths. Negative thoughts typically focus on three key areas: oneself, the world, and the future. A depressed person may feel worthless, see the world as a hostile or unjust place, and believe that the future is bleak and hopeless. This way of thinking is known as the cognitive triad of depression, a concept developed by psychologist Aaron Beck, the founder of cognitive-behavioral therapy.

The constant repetition of these thoughts not only reinforces depression but also prevents the person from seeing solutions to their problems or experiencing positive emotions. Learning to identify and challenge this type of negative self-talk is a crucial step in treating depression.

4.2. The Trap of Learned Helplessness

Another important psychological factor in depression is learned helplessness, a concept developed by psychologist Martin Seligman in the 1960s. This term refers to the belief that, no matter what a person does, they cannot change their situation. As a result, the person gives up and stops trying to improve their life, which perpetuates the depressive state.

Learned helplessness often arises after repeated experiences of failure or traumatic situations. If a person has tried multiple times to improve their life without success, they may begin to believe that nothing they do will change their reality. This can manifest in phrases like:

- "Why bother? Nothing will change."

- "Everything I do goes wrong."

This attitude of surrender not only affects the person's ability to find solutions to their problems but also reinforces feelings of powerlessness and hopelessness, fundamental pillars of depression.

It is important to understand that learned helplessness is not an objective reality but a perception that can be modified. In cognitive-behavioral therapy, efforts are made to dismantle these limiting beliefs and help people regain a sense of control over their lives.

4.3. Cognitive-Behavioral Therapy: How to Transform Our Mind

Cognitive-behavioral therapy (CBT) is one of the most effective treatments for depression. It is based on the idea that our thoughts, emotions, and behaviors are interconnected and that by changing the way we think, we can positively influence our emotions and actions.

In CBT, the goal is to identify the negative automatic thoughts that contribute to depression. Once identified, these thoughts are challenged and replaced with more realistic and constructive beliefs. The process of change involves several steps:

1. **Identifying Negative Thoughts:** The first step is learning to recognize the negative automatic thoughts that arise in everyday situations. Often, these thoughts occur so quickly and automatically that we are not even aware of them.

2. **Challenging the Thoughts:** Once the negative thoughts are identified, the next step is to challenge them. Are they really true? Is there evidence to support these thoughts? This process helps dismantle irrational beliefs and see situations from a more balanced perspective.

3. **Cognitive Restructuring:** After challenging the negative

thoughts, the focus shifts to replacing them with more realistic and helpful beliefs. For example, instead of thinking "I'm useless," a more constructive belief might be, "Sometimes I make mistakes, but I also have many skills and strengths."

4. **Behavioral Change:** As thoughts transform, behavior also changes. People with depression often avoid activities due to pessimism and lack of motivation. CBT helps individuals break the cycle of avoidance and re-engage in activities they once enjoyed, which contributes to improving their mood.

4.4. Practical Exercise: Thought Journal and Cognitive Restructuring

A very useful exercise for combating negative self-talk is keeping a thought journal. This journal will help you identify the automatic thoughts that fuel your depression and restructure them in a more constructive way. Here are the steps to follow:

1. **Identify Negative Thoughts:**
    Throughout the day, write down moments when you feel particularly bad, whether sad, anxious, or hopeless. Note the context and, most importantly, the automatic thoughts that arose at that moment. Don't worry about judging whether they are right or wrong at this point—just write them down.

Example: "Today I had an argument with my boss. I thought: 'I always mess everything up, I'll never measure up.'"

2. **Challenge the Thoughts:**
    Once you have written down your negative thoughts, ask yourself if those thoughts are really true. Is there evidence to support them? Are they rational or distorted? This step is crucial for starting to challenge the automatic beliefs that perpetuate depression.

Questions to Challenge Your Thoughts:

- o   What evidence do I have that this thought is true?

- o   Am I jumping to conclusions?

- o   Am I seeing things in absolute terms (all or nothing)?

Example: "It's true that I made a mistake at work, but that doesn't mean I mess everything up. I've succeeded in other projects, and my boss has praised me in the past."

3. **Restructuring the Thought:**
    Once you've challenged your negative thoughts, try replacing them with a more balanced and realistic interpretation of the situation. This new thought should be more rational and based on evidence.

Example: "I made a mistake today, but that doesn't define my overall ability. I've learned from this mistake and can improve."

4. **Track Your Progress:**
    Keeping a daily record of these exercises will allow you to observe your progress over time. As you continue challenging and restructuring your thoughts, you should begin to notice an improvement in your mood and your ability to manage difficult situations.

Here's a sample format for your thought journal:

Situation	Automatic Thought	Emotion	Thought Challenge	Restructured Thought
Argument with boss	"I always mess everything up."	Sadness	I've done things well before. It's just one mistake.	"I made a mistake, but I've also had successes at work."
Flight cancellation	"Nobody wants to spend time with me."	Loneliness	My friends have other responsibilities; it doesn't mean they don't care.	"My friends value me; they're just busy today."

This exercise is a powerful tool to help you become aware of how your thoughts influence your emotions and behavior, and it provides a practical way to begin breaking the negative cycle.

As you progress in this process, you will realize that while we can't control everything that happens in our lives, we can learn to manage how we interpret and respond to difficulties. Cognitive-behavioral therapy, along with practical exercises like the thought journal, empowers us to take control of our minds and, over time, transform our emotional experience.

Chapter 4: Social and Cultural Factors

Depression is not only influenced by biological and psychological aspects, but also by social and cultural factors. The relationships we maintain with others, societal expectations, and the way society perceives depression have a profound impact on how we experience and cope with the illness. This chapter explores how the social and cultural environment can affect both the development and recovery from depression, from the role of family and friends to the stigma that still surrounds this condition.

4.1. The Role of Family and Friends in Depression

The support network provided by family and friends plays a crucial role in how a person with depression faces their illness. A positive and understanding family environment can be a great relief, while a lack of support or understanding can exacerbate symptoms and make recovery more difficult.

- **Emotional support:** For someone suffering from depression, having loved ones who offer genuine emotional support can make a world of difference. The feeling of being heard and understood alleviates some of the loneliness that often accompanies depression. However, it's important that the support is not just comforting words but is also accompanied by empathy and patience.

- **Lack of understanding:** Often, family members or friends, due to a lack of knowledge, may underestimate the severity of depression or suggest simplistic solutions like "You just need to try harder" or "Go out and have fun." These reactions, while well-intentioned, can make the person with depression feel misunderstood or guilty for not improving.

- **Intervention and professional help:** Family and friends can also play a key role in encouraging the person to seek professional help. Sometimes, the person with depression lacks the energy or clarity to take that step, and having someone close to guide them to a psychologist or psychiatrist can be crucial.

Thus, relationships can act as either a protective or risk factor in the depression process. While friends and family cannot "cure" depression, they can provide the necessary support environment for the person to feel accompanied in their struggle.

4.2. Social Stigma and How to Face It

Despite advances in understanding mental health, the stigma associated with depression remains strong in many cultures. This stigma not only perpetuates harmful myths but also prevents many people from seeking the help they need.

- **Shame and silence:** One of the most harmful effects of stigma is that many people who suffer from depression feel ashamed to openly talk about what they are experiencing. The fear of being seen as "weak" or "incapable" leads many to hide their symptoms, delaying or preventing treatment.

- **Stereotypes and prejudice:** There is a mistaken belief that depression is simply a lack of willpower or an excuse to avoid responsibilities. This type of prejudice reinforces the idea that depression is something one can overcome on their own, adding pressure to those suffering from it and leading them to feel guilty for not being able to improve.

- **How to face it:** The first step in combating stigma is education. The more we understand about depression and its causes, the more we can dismantle the erroneous beliefs surrounding it. Awareness campaigns and the visibility of public figures openly discussing their struggle with depression have helped reduce stigma, but much remains to be done at both the personal and community levels.

For those suffering from depression, confronting stigma can be an additional challenge. However, speaking openly about the illness with trusted people and seeking support networks in therapy groups or the community can be a first step toward breaking that social isolation.

4.3. Social Media and Its Influence on Self-Esteem

In the digital age, social media has become a central part of our lives. While it can serve as a tool for connecting with friends and loved ones, it can also negatively impact mental health, particularly in relation to self-esteem and depression.

- **Constant comparison:** Social media often portrays an idealized version of people's lives, leading to constant and damaging comparisons. Seeing only the positive aspects of others' lives can make people with depression feel even more inadequate or lonely. This is exacerbated when they are already struggling with low self-esteem and believe their lives are inferior to those of others.

- **Seeking validation:** For some, the pursuit of "likes" or positive comments on social media becomes a form of external validation. This can be dangerous because self-esteem becomes tied to external and volatile factors, such as online approval. A lack of interaction or negative responses can make a person with depression feel even more rejected or invisible.

- **Cyberbullying and toxicity:** Social media can also be a space where bullying and toxicity are perpetuated. Negative comments, teasing, or open criticism can worsen feelings of low self-esteem and hopelessness in those already dealing with mental illness.

- **Coping strategies:** One way to reduce the negative impact of social media is to limit its use or curate the content you are exposed to. Following accounts that promote positivity, authenticity, and mental health can help create a healthier digital environment. Additionally, it's important to remember that what is shown on social media is not a complete representation of a person's life, but rather an edited version.

4.4. Case Study: Laura and the Impact of Social Media on Her Well-Being

Laura, a 27-year-old woman, began noticing changes in her mood after several months of being unemployed. She felt increasingly unmotivated and lonely, but what affected her the most was the time she spent on social media. While looking for a job, she spent hours scrolling through Instagram, seeing her friends share photos of their jobs, vacations, and personal achievements.

She often compared herself to them, thinking, "What have I done wrong? Why does everyone seem to have a perfect life, and I'm stuck?" Over time, these negative thoughts became more frequent and deep, and Laura began isolating herself from her real-life friends, avoiding socializing or maintaining conversations because she felt inadequate.

At first, Laura didn't connect her social media use with her mood, but after speaking with a therapist, she realized how constant comparison was affecting her self-esteem. Her therapist suggested a few changes:

- **Limiting time on social media:** Laura decided to set a daily time limit for social media use, spending fewer hours aimlessly browsing.

- **Curating her follower list:** She unfollowed accounts that made her feel worse about herself and started following profiles that shared positive messages about mental health and self-acceptance.

- **Engaging in offline activities:** Instead of spending so much time on social media, Laura began engaging in activities that made her feel good, such as painting and reading, and she joined a local art group where she met new people outside the digital environment.

Over time, Laura noticed an improvement in her mood. By reducing her exposure to constant comparison on social media and reconnecting with activities she enjoyed, she began to rebuild her self-esteem.

This case shows how social media, when not managed properly, can exacerbate feelings of inadequacy and depression. However, it also highlights that making conscious changes in how we interact with technology can positively impact our emotional well-being.

nal

Chapter 5: Diagnosing Depression

The diagnosis of depression is a crucial process that allows for proper identification of the disorder and the commencement of treatment as soon as possible. Often, depression goes undiagnosed or is misinterpreted, preventing individuals from receiving the help they need. In this chapter, we will explore how mental health professionals assess and diagnose depression, the tools they use, and the differences between depression and other mood disorders. Additionally, we include a practical exercise to help you reflect on your own symptoms and, if necessary, seek help.

6.1. Clinical Evaluation: How Depression Is Diagnosed

The diagnosis of depression is primarily made through a clinical evaluation conducted by a mental health professional, such as a psychologist or psychiatrist. The evaluation begins with a detailed interview that explores the patient's emotional, physical, and behavioral symptoms, as well as their medical and family history.

For a diagnosis of major depressive disorder to be made, the symptoms must be present for at least two consecutive weeks and must represent a significant change from the person's previous state. The most widely used diagnostic criteria are those established by the *Diagnostic and Statistical Manual of Mental Disorders* (DSM-5), which includes the following key symptoms:

- Depressed mood most of the day, nearly every day

- Loss of interest or pleasure in most daily activities

- Significant changes in weight or appetite

- Insomnia or hypersomnia (excessive sleep)

- Fatigue or lack of energy nearly every day

- Feelings of worthlessness or excessive guilt

- Difficulty concentrating or making decisions

- Recurrent thoughts of death or suicide

During the evaluation, the professional will also inquire about risk factors such as a family history of depression, previous episodes of the illness, trauma, or recent stressful events, such as the loss of a loved one or work problems.

It is essential that the diagnosis be made by a qualified professional, as many symptoms of depression overlap with other mental or physical disorders, and a misdiagnosis can lead to inadequate treatment.

6.2. Diagnostic Tools: Questionnaires and Interviews

In addition to the clinical interview, there are various diagnostic tools that can help professionals assess the severity of depression and other aspects related to the patient's mental state. Some of the most commonly used tools include:

- **Patient Health Questionnaire (PHQ-9):** This is one of the most common tests to assess the severity of depression. It consists of nine questions measuring the frequency of depressive symptoms over the past two weeks. The PHQ-9 is quick to administer and very useful for tracking symptoms throughout treatment.

- **Beck Depression Inventory (BDI):** Developed by psychologist Aaron Beck, this questionnaire contains 21 items that assess the intensity of depression. It includes questions about emotional, physical, and cognitive symptoms such as sadness, hopelessness, fatigue, and self-esteem.

- **Structured Clinical Interview for DSM-5 (SCID):** This is a more exhaustive tool used by mental health professionals to make a precise diagnosis. It allows for the evaluation of not only depression but also the possible presence of other psychiatric disorders.

- **Hamilton Depression Rating Scale (HDRS):** Similar to the previous tools, the HDRS is a questionnaire that assesses the severity of depressive symptoms, but in this case, the clinician administers the questions and scores them, evaluating aspects such as mood, changes in sleep, and levels of agitation.

These tools are used as support in the diagnosis, but they do not replace clinical judgment. They are helpful in complementing the initial interview and for monitoring the patient's progress throughout treatment.

6.3. Differences Between Depression and Other Mood Disorders

It is important to distinguish depression from other mood disorders, as some of them can share similar symptoms, which may lead to confusion for both patients and professionals. Below, we review some of the most common disorders that can be confused with depression:

- **Bipolar Disorder:** Formerly known as manic-depressive disorder, bipolar disorder involves extreme mood swings, alternating between episodes of depression and episodes of mania or hypomania (euphoria, high energy, or irritability). During depressive episodes, the symptoms can be very similar to major depression, but it is crucial to identify the manic episodes for a correct diagnosis.

- **Dysthymia (Persistent Depressive Disorder):** Dysthymia is a milder but chronic form of depression. The symptoms may not be as severe as in major depression, but they typically last for at least two years. People with dysthymia often feel sad or unmotivated constantly, but they continue to function in their daily lives, albeit with a reduced quality of life.

- **Generalized Anxiety Disorder (GAD):** Although depression and anxiety are distinct disorders, many people with depression also suffer from anxiety, and the symptoms can overlap. While depression is characterized primarily by hopelessness and lack of energy, anxiety involves excessive worry and constant tension. A careful diagnosis is necessary to identify which disorder predominates or if both coexist.

- **Seasonal Affective Disorder (SAD):** SAD is a type of depression that occurs mainly during the winter months, when there is less sunlight. The symptoms usually disappear in spring or summer. It is important to distinguish SAD from major depression, as treatment may include specific therapies such as light therapy.

- **Post-Traumatic Stress Disorder (PTSD):** PTSD can share some symptoms with depression, such as loss of interest in activities, social withdrawal, and deep sadness. However, PTSD originates from a traumatic event and usually includes flashbacks, nightmares, and an exaggerated startle response, which distinguishes it from major depression.

A correct diagnosis is essential, as each of these disorders has different treatment approaches, and confusing them could lead to ineffective or inappropriate therapies.

6.4. Practical Exercise: Self-Assessment of Depressive Symptoms

Conducting a self-assessment can help you identify if you are experiencing depressive symptoms and whether you should consider seeking professional help. Below is a simple exercise that you can perform to reflect on your own symptoms. Respond to each question with the frequency with which you have experienced the following symptoms in the past two weeks.

Self-Assessment of Depressive Symptoms (Based on the PHQ-9):

- Have you felt depressed, sad, or hopeless most of the day, nearly every day?
    - ( ) Never
    - ( ) Some days
    - ( ) More than half the days
    - ( ) Nearly every day
- Have you lost interest or pleasure in doing things you used to enjoy?
    - ( ) Never
    - ( ) Some days
    - ( ) More than half the days
    - ( ) Nearly every day
- Have you had trouble falling asleep or woken up frequently during the night?
    - ( ) Never
    - ( ) Some days
    - ( ) More than half the days
    - ( ) Nearly every day
- Have you felt tired or had little energy?
    - ( ) Never
    - ( ) Some days
    - ( ) More than half the days

- o ( ) Nearly every day

- Have you felt bad about yourself or that you have failed, or that you are a failure?

  - o ( ) Never

  - o ( ) Some days

  - o ( ) More than half the days

  - o ( ) Nearly every day

- Have you had difficulty concentrating, for example, when reading or watching TV?

  - o ( ) Never

  - o ( ) Some days

  - o ( ) More than half the days

  - o ( ) Nearly every day

- Have you had little appetite or overeaten?

  - o ( ) Never

  - o ( ) Some days

  - o ( ) More than half the days

  - o ( ) Nearly every day

- Have you had thoughts that you would be better off dead or thoughts of hurting yourself?

  - o ( ) Never

  - o ( ) Some days

  - o ( ) More than half the days

  - o ( ) Nearly every day

Interpretation of Results:

- If you have marked "More than half the days" or "Nearly every day" for several of these questions, you may be experiencing depressive symptoms, and it would be advisable to consult with a mental health professional for a more detailed evaluation.

- If you answered affirmatively to the question about suicidal thoughts, it is important that you seek immediate help, either by contacting a doctor, psychologist, or an emergency helpline.

This exercise does not replace a professional evaluation, but it can serve as an initial guide to recognizing whether the symptoms you are experiencing may be related to depression.

This chapter has explored how depression is diagnosed, from clinical evaluation and diagnostic tools to differentiating it from other mood disorders. The key to an accurate diagnosis lies in the combination of a careful professional evaluation and the use of reliable tools to measure the severity and nature of the symptoms. Better understanding your emotional state and conducting a self-assessment can help you take the first step toward the appropriate treatment.

Chapter 6: Pharmacological Treatments

Pharmacological treatment is one of the most common options for managing depression and has proven effective in many cases, especially when combined with psychological therapy. However, antidepressant medications still generate doubts, fears, and myths that often cause people to hesitate before starting treatment. In this chapter, we will explore the types of available antidepressants, their side effects, how the right treatment is chosen, and debunk some misconceptions about medication. We will also present a case study to illustrate the real process of someone receiving pharmacological treatment.

6.1. Antidepressants: Types, Side Effects, and Effectiveness

Antidepressants are medications designed to correct imbalances in neurotransmitters, the brain's chemicals that influence mood. There are several types of antidepressants, each with its characteristics, side effects, and levels of effectiveness. Below are the most common types:

- **Selective Serotonin Reuptake Inhibitors (SSRIs):** SSRIs are the most commonly prescribed type of antidepressant due to their effectiveness and relatively few side effects compared to others. SSRIs increase the amount of serotonin in the brain, a chemical that regulates mood. Examples of SSRIs include escitalopram, fluoxetine, and sertraline.

Side effects: These may include nausea, insomnia, loss of appetite, decreased libido, and dry mouth. Often, these effects decrease as the body adjusts to the medication.

- **Serotonin and Norepinephrine Reuptake Inhibitors (SNRIs):** Medications like venlafaxine and duloxetine act on both serotonin and norepinephrine, another neurotransmitter involved in regulating mood and stress.

Side effects: Similar to those of SSRIs but can include increased blood pressure in some cases.

- **Tricyclic Antidepressants:** These were the first antidepressants developed but are now prescribed less frequently due to their more pronounced side effects. However, they are still effective in certain cases that are resistant to other treatments. Examples include amitriptyline and nortriptyline.

Side effects: These may include drowsiness, weight gain, blurred vision, and dizziness.

- **Monoamine Oxidase Inhibitors (MAOIs):** These are less common due to necessary dietary restrictions and potential serious side effects, but they can be helpful in some difficult-to-treat cases. MAOIs like phenelzine work by inhibiting an enzyme that breaks down neurotransmitters like serotonin, dopamine, and norepinephrine.

Side effects: Can interact dangerously with certain foods and medications and cause dizziness, insomnia, and high blood pressure.

- **Atypical Antidepressants:** This group includes medications like bupropion, which works on dopamine and norepinephrine. Bupropion is often prescribed when SSRIs or SNRIs are not effective or if the patient experiences side effects such as reduced sexual desire.

Side effects: Insomnia, dry mouth, anxiety, and irritability.

Effectiveness: Antidepressants do not usually work immediately. It can take between 2 and 6 weeks for a person to notice a significant improvement. The effectiveness of antidepressants varies between individuals, and it may be necessary to adjust the dose or change the medication if the first one is not effective.

6.2. How to Choose the Right Treatment

Choosing the right antidepressant is a process that should be done in consultation with a doctor, usually a psychiatrist, who will evaluate the patient's symptoms, medical history, and other factors before prescribing a specific medication. The following factors influence the choice of treatment:

- **Severity of symptoms:** Antidepressants are more often recommended for moderate or severe cases of depression. For mild cases, other forms of treatment, such as psychotherapy or lifestyle changes, may be tried first.

- **Previous response to medications:** If a person has taken antidepressants in the past and responded well to a particular drug, the doctor may prescribe the same medication or a similar one.

- **Side effects:** Since side effects can vary from person to person, the doctor will consider the side effect profile of each medication. For example, if the patient experiences insomnia, the doctor may opt for an antidepressant that also helps with sleep.

- **Underlying medical conditions:** People with other medical conditions (such as hypertension, heart problems, or diabetes) need to take extra precautions, as some antidepressants can worsen certain conditions. The doctor will also check for possible interactions with other medications the patient is taking.

- **Personal factors:** The patient's preferences and lifestyle also play an important role. For example, if the person experiences anxiety or insomnia, a sedative medication may be chosen. If decreased sexual desire is an issue, the doctor may opt for a drug that minimizes this effect.

- **Continuous monitoring:** Once an antidepressant is chosen, regular follow-up with the doctor is important to assess how the patient responds to treatment. In some cases, it may be necessary to switch medications or adjust the dose for better results or to minimize side effects.

6.3. Myths About Medication and How to Address Them

Antidepressant medications are surrounded by various myths that can dissuade people from starting or continuing treatment. Below, we address some of the most common myths and clarify the realities behind them:

- **Myth 1: "Antidepressants will change my personality."**
  Reality: Antidepressants do not change a person's personality. Their role is to alleviate depressive symptoms and restore chemical balance in the brain. Instead of changing who you are, antidepressants help you feel more like yourself again, without the constant burden of depression.

- **Myth 2: "If I take antidepressants, I will become dependent or addicted."**
  Reality: Antidepressants do not cause addiction. Unlike other substances, they do not trigger cravings or compulsive behaviors. However, it is important not to stop taking antidepressants abruptly, as this can cause withdrawal symptoms. Always follow your doctor's instructions to taper off gradually if necessary.

- **Myth 3: "Only very severe cases need antidepressants."**
  Reality: Antidepressants are not only for severe cases of depression. Depending on the symptoms and individual

needs, they can be helpful in a wide range of cases, from moderate to severe, and in combination with other treatments like therapy.

- **Myth 4: "Antidepressants work immediately."**
  Reality: As mentioned earlier, antidepressants can take several weeks to take effect. Many people expect to feel better within a few days, but it is important to be patient and allow the medication to work over time.

- **Myth 5: "If I start taking antidepressants, I will have to take them for life."**
  Reality: Not everyone who takes antidepressants needs to continue them indefinitely. Some people may benefit from temporary treatment, while others may need long-term treatment. The duration of treatment depends on the severity and nature of the depression and is decided in consultation with the doctor.

6.4. Case Study: Marcos and His Experience With Pharmacological Treatment

Marcos, a 35-year-old man, had been feeling overwhelmed by sadness and fatigue for several months. Although he had tried to cope with the situation on his own, his symptoms worsened. Finally, after talking to his primary care doctor, he was referred to a psychiatrist, who diagnosed Marcos with moderate depression.

During the initial consultation, the psychiatrist explained the available treatment options. Since Marcos had been struggling with insomnia and low energy, the psychiatrist prescribed an SSRI that would not only regulate his serotonin levels but also help improve his sleep. It was also agreed to combine the pharmacological treatment with cognitive-behavioral therapy (CBT) to address the negative thoughts fueling his depression.

The first few weeks were not easy for Marcos. A few days after starting the medication, he experienced some side effects such as mild nausea and loss of appetite, but the psychiatrist had warned him that this was normal and that the symptoms should subside over time. As the weeks passed, Marcos noticed that his sleep improved and that he no longer felt as fatigued during the day. Additionally, therapy was helping him identify and modify the negative thoughts that were weighing him down.

After two months of treatment, Marcos began to feel more optimistic and motivated. Although not every day was perfect, his symptoms had significantly decreased. He continued treatment for several more months, with regular check-ups with the psychiatrist to adjust the dosage as needed.

Finally, after about a year of treatment, Marcos and his psychiatrist decided it was time to start gradually reducing the antidepressant dose, always under medical supervision. The transition was gradual and smooth, and although Marcos continued participating in therapy, he no longer needed medication to maintain his well-being.

Marcos' case illustrates how pharmacological treatment can be a valuable tool in managing depression when combined with proper follow-up and other forms of support, such as psychotherapy. The key to success lies in patience, medical supervision, and combining approaches to address all aspects of the illness.

Chapter 7: Effective Psychological Therapies

The treatment of depression is not limited solely to the use of medication. Psychological therapies are fundamental in addressing the emotional and cognitive factors that perpetuate the disorder. Over the years, various forms of therapy have proven effective in helping individuals manage their symptoms, change thought and behavior patterns, and regain emotional well-being. In this chapter, we will explore three particularly useful therapeutic approaches: Cognitive Behavioral Therapy (CBT), Acceptance and Commitment Therapy (ACT), and mindfulness. We also include a practical mindfulness-based exercise to help manage depression.

7.1. Cognitive Behavioral Therapy (CBT)

Cognitive Behavioral Therapy is one of the most widely used and effective therapies for treating depression. It is based on the idea that our thoughts, emotions, and behaviors are interconnected, and by changing our thought patterns, we can improve our emotional health and, in turn, our behavior.

The primary goal of CBT is to help individuals identify and modify the automatic negative thoughts that contribute to depression. These thoughts are often distorted and irrational, but they are so habitual that we often don't even notice them. CBT teaches individuals to challenge these thoughts and replace them with more realistic and constructive beliefs.

How does CBT work?

The process begins with identifying negative thoughts. Through self-observation and therapy, the patient learns to recognize the automatic thoughts that arise in various situations, such as "I'm not good enough" or "I'll never be happy." From there, the therapist helps challenge these thoughts. Are they really true? What evidence supports or refutes them? Finally, work is done to replace them with more realistic thoughts, such as "Sometimes I make mistakes, but that doesn't define my worth."

Key components of CBT:

- **Cognitive restructuring:** The process of identifying and changing negative thoughts.

- **Gradual exposure:** Facing situations that are avoided due to fear or anxiety progressively, with the goal of reducing avoidance.

- **Coping strategies:** Techniques to deal more effectively with stressful or difficult situations.

CBT also emphasizes behavioral changes, as depression often leads to inactivity or avoidance of activities that usually bring pleasure or satisfaction. The therapist encourages the patient to reintroduce these activities into their life, even if they don't feel like doing them at first, knowing that, over time, this can improve their mood.

7.2. Acceptance and Commitment Therapy (ACT)

Acceptance and Commitment Therapy is another effective form of treating depression. Unlike CBT, which focuses on changing negative thoughts, ACT promotes the acceptance of these thoughts and emotions instead of fighting them. The premise of ACT is that trying to avoid or control painful thoughts and emotions often worsens the problem. Instead, ACT teaches individuals to live fully, even in the presence of difficult emotions or thoughts.

The purpose of ACT is to help people free themselves from the internal struggle with their negative thoughts and emotions and commit to actions that align with their deepest values. This is achieved through two main components:

- **Acceptance:** Instead of avoiding or trying to change

uncomfortable thoughts and feelings, ACT teaches individuals to accept them. It acknowledges that these emotions are part of the human experience and that fighting them only intensifies the discomfort.

- **Commitment to action:** ACT emphasizes the importance of taking concrete steps based on personal values. This means identifying what is truly important to the individual (family, relationships, work, personal growth) and committing to actions that promote these values, even if negative thoughts persist.

ACT uses techniques such as **cognitive defusion**, which helps individuals distance themselves from their thoughts and see them simply as words or mental images, and mindfulness, which allows one to stay present in the moment and accept experiences as they are, without judgment.

7.3. Mindfulness: Being Present to Heal

Mindfulness is a practice that has gained popularity in recent years as an effective tool for combating depression. It is based on the idea of being fully present in the current moment, without judging the emotions or thoughts that arise, nor trying to change them. Although it has roots in Buddhist meditation, mindfulness has been adapted and is widely used in psychology as a technique to improve emotional well-being.

People with depression often get caught in cycles of negative thoughts about the past or worries about the future. Mindfulness helps break this cycle by training the mind to focus on the present and accept emotions and thoughts as they are, without trying to avoid or resist them.

Benefits of mindfulness:

- **Stress reduction:** Helps reduce stress responses and decrease the emotional intensity of negative thoughts.

- **Improved concentration:** By training the mind to focus on the here and now, it can improve concentration and decision-making abilities.

- **Greater self-acceptance:** Encourages an attitude of kindness and acceptance toward oneself, which is crucial for overcoming feelings of guilt or low self-esteem.

Mindfulness-Based Cognitive Therapy (MBCT) combines CBT with mindfulness and has proven effective in preventing relapses in people with recurrent depression. By integrating these practices, MBCT helps individuals change their relationship with depressive thoughts, rather than trying to eliminate them.

7.4. Practical Exercise: Mindfulness Techniques for Depression

Below is a practical mindfulness exercise that you can use in your daily life to manage depression symptoms. This exercise focuses on **breath awareness**, a simple yet powerful technique that helps calm the mind and connect you to the present moment.

Breath Awareness Exercise:

1. **Find a quiet place:** Sit in a comfortable position, either in a chair or on the floor. Close your eyes if you feel comfortable doing so.

2. **Focus on your breathing:** Begin to pay attention to your breath. Notice how the air enters and exits your body. Don't try to change your breathing—simply observe it as it is.

3. **Notice the sensations:** Focus on the sensations of the breath. Feel the air passing through your nostrils, filling your lungs, and then leaving your body.

4. **Stay present:** If your mind starts to wander, gently bring

your attention back to your breath without judging yourself for being distracted. The goal is not to empty your mind but to train it to return to the present whenever it gets lost in thoughts.

5. **Practice for 5-10 minutes:** Start with a short session and gradually increase the time as you become more comfortable with the practice.

This exercise can be practiced at any time of day, especially during moments of stress, sadness, or anxiety. By focusing on the breath, you can anchor your attention to the present and create a sense of calm, helping to break the cycle of negative thoughts associated with depression.

Chapter 8: Self-Care Strategies

Self-care is an essential component in the treatment and management of depression. Maintaining healthy habits in areas such as sleep, nutrition, exercise, and stress management can significantly improve emotional well-being. In this chapter, we will explore how to implement effective self-care strategies, how to structure a personalized plan, and the importance of incorporating relaxation and breathing techniques into daily life. At the end, we offer a practical exercise to help you develop your own weekly self-care plan.

8.1. The Importance of Healthy Habits: Sleep, Nutrition, and Exercise

Daily habits have a direct impact on our physical and emotional well-being. Self-care in the context of depression includes basic aspects that are often neglected due to fatigue or lack of motivation, but which are crucial for improving mood. The three pillars of self-care are sleep, nutrition, and exercise.

- **Sleep:** Adequate rest is essential for mental health. Sleep disturbances, such as insomnia or oversleeping, are common symptoms of depression, but they can also worsen it.

Sleeping between 7 and 9 hours each night helps regulate energy levels and cognitive functions. Establishing a consistent sleep routine, avoiding electronic devices before bed, and creating a calm environment are key steps to improving sleep quality.

- **Nutrition:** What we eat directly affects brain function. A diet rich in processed foods, refined sugars, and saturated fats can increase fatigue and a general sense of malaise. On the other hand, a balanced diet with plenty of fruits, vegetables, lean proteins, and healthy fats (such as omega-3 from fatty fish) promotes the production of neurotransmitters like serotonin, which regulate mood. Staying well-hydrated is also crucial for mental health.

- **Exercise:** Regular physical activity has highly positive effects on mental health. Aerobic exercises such as walking, swimming, or cycling stimulate the release of endorphins and improve serotonin and dopamine levels, helping to combat depression. It is not necessary to engage in intense exercises; even a 20-30 minute walk each day can positively impact mood. Additionally, exercise improves sleep and reduces stress.

8.2. How to Structure a Self-Care Plan

A self-care plan is a personal tool that helps you organize activities and habits that promote your physical, mental, and emotional well-being. This plan does not have to be complicated or demanding, but it should be tailored to your needs and goals. Here's how to structure it in a few steps:

1. **Assess your current needs:** Make a list of the areas in your life that you think need more attention. Are you getting enough sleep? Are you eating well? Do you take time to

relax? Identifying areas that need care will help you prioritize your efforts.

2. **Set realistic goals:** You don't need to make drastic changes right away. Set small, achievable goals. For example, if you want to improve your diet, aim to incorporate more fruits and vegetables into your daily meals or gradually reduce processed foods. If you want to exercise, start with activities you enjoy.

3. **Create a routine:** Consistency is key to self-care. Try to schedule regular activities into your daily or weekly routine. For example, you can set a fixed sleep schedule, plan meals ahead of time to ensure they're nutritious, and set aside time for exercise or relaxation.

4. **Include emotional well-being activities:** Self-care isn't just about physical health, but also emotional well-being. Make time for activities that make you feel good, like reading, spending time with friends, practicing gratitude, or simply relaxing in a peaceful space.

5. **Track your progress:** Keeping a record of your self-care plan helps you evaluate your progress and adjust your approach if necessary. This will help you stay motivated and become aware of the benefits you're gaining.

8.3. Relaxation and Breathing Techniques to Combat Stress

Stress is a key factor that worsens depression. Learning to manage stress effectively is crucial for self-care. Below are some relaxation and breathing techniques that can help reduce tension and improve emotional well-being.

- **Diaphragmatic breathing:** Also known as abdominal breathing, this technique involves inhaling deeply using the diaphragm, helping to lower the heart rate and promote relaxation. To practice it, sit or lie in a comfortable position, placing one hand on your abdomen and the other on your chest. Inhale deeply through your nose, making sure the hand on your abdomen rises while the hand on your chest remains still. Exhale slowly through your mouth, fully emptying your lungs. Repeat this cycle for 5 to 10 minutes.

- **4-7-8 breathing technique:** This technique is designed to induce relaxation. It involves inhaling for 4 seconds, holding the breath for 7 seconds, and exhaling slowly for 8 seconds. This method has been shown to reduce stress levels and help with sleep.

- **Progressive muscle relaxation:** In this exercise, you tense and then relax different muscle groups in the body, helping to release accumulated physical tension. Start with your feet and work your way up to your head. Tense each muscle group for 5 seconds and then fully relax it, noticing the difference between tension and relaxation.

- **Guided visualization:** This technique involves closing your eyes and imagining a place or situation that brings you peace and tranquility. It could be a natural landscape, a beach, or any place where you feel safe and relaxed. Visualize every detail, from the sounds to the colors, to make the experience as real as possible. Visualization helps disconnect from stressful thoughts and fosters a sense of calm.

8.4. Practical Exercise: Personal Weekly Self-Care Plan

The following exercise will guide you in creating your own weekly self-care plan. Throughout the week, you will track your self-care habits and activities in the areas of sleep, nutrition, exercise, relaxation, and emotional well-being. At the end of the week, you will review your progress and adjust your plan if necessary.

Step 1: Plan Your Week

In a notebook or chart, organize your week by dividing the days into sections (morning, afternoon, evening) and add the self-care activities you plan to do. Below is an example of how to structure your plan:

Day	Sleep (Hours)	Nutrition (Goals)	Exercise (Minutes)	Relaxation/Breathing (Minutes)	Emotional Well-being (Activity)
Monday	7-8 hours	Eat 2 fruits and 3 vegetables	30 minutes walking	10 minutes breathing	Read a favorite book
Tuesday	7-8 hours	Drink 8 glasses of water	20 minutes yoga	15 minutes visualization	Chat with a friend
Wednesday	7-8 hours	Avoid processed foods	30 minutes cycling	10 minutes breathing	Listen to relaxing music
Thursday	7-8 hours	Eat fish or nuts	30 minutes walking	10 minutes muscle relaxation	Write in a journal
Friday	7-8 hours	Have a balanced meal	20 minutes stretching	15 minutes breathing	Watch a pleasant movie
Saturday	7-8 hours	Eat more lean proteins	30 minutes walking	10 minutes breathing	Spend time outdoors
Sunday	7-8 hours	Plan meals	20 minutes yoga	10 minutes breathing	Guided meditation

At the end of each day, note which activities you completed and how you felt. Evaluate whether you met your self-care goals and whether you noticed any changes in your mood or overall well-being.

Step 3: Weekly Reflection

At the end of the week, reflect on the following questions:

- Which activities made you feel better physically and emotionally?

- What challenges did you encounter in following the plan?

- What could you adjust for the next week?

This self-care plan will help you regularly integrate healthy habits into your life, allowing you to observe how changes in your daily routine influence your overall well-being.

This chapter has covered the importance of healthy habits in treating depression and how to structure a personalized self-care plan. We've also explored relaxation and breathing techniques that can help manage stress, and provided a practical exercise to create your own weekly self-care plan. Incorporating these strategies into your daily life can be key to improving your mood and long-term well-being.

Chapter 9: The Impact of Physical Exercise on Depression

Physical exercise not only benefits the body but also has a profound impact on mental well-being. Numerous studies have shown that regular physical activity can improve symptoms of depression and prevent relapses. In this chapter, we will explore how exercise regulates mood, the types of exercise most recommended for people with depression, and how it can act as a preventive tool. We will also examine the case of Ana, who found sports to be a path to recovery.

9.1. How Exercise Regulates Mood

Physical exercise directly affects the brain, influencing the neurotransmitters that regulate mood. When we exercise, the body releases several chemicals that contribute to improved emotional well-being:

- **Endorphins:** Known as the "happiness hormones," endorphins are released during exercise and produce feelings of pleasure and pain relief. This is often described as the "runner's high" or the feeling of well-being after intense physical activity.
- **Serotonin:** Physical exercise also increases serotonin levels, a neurotransmitter that regulates mood, sleep, and appetite. Low levels of serotonin are associated with depression, and exercise helps maintain these levels in balance.

- **Dopamine:** This substance is linked to motivation and pleasure. Regular exercise increases dopamine levels, which can counteract apathy and anhedonia (the inability to feel pleasure), two common symptoms of depression.
- **Neurogenesis:** Some studies suggest that exercise can promote the growth of new neurons in the hippocampus, a brain region involved in mood regulation and memory. Depression is often associated with a reduction in the size of the hippocampus, and exercise may help reverse this effect.

In addition to its chemical effects, exercise has psychological benefits. The sense of accomplishment after completing physical activity can boost self-esteem and foster greater self-confidence. Additionally, simply moving can distract the mind from negative thoughts and improve mental clarity.

9.2. Recommended Types of Exercise for People with Depression

Not all exercises are the same, and it's important to choose those that suit the individual's needs and capabilities. For people with depression, the most important thing is that exercise is accessible, enjoyable, and sustainable over time. Here are some recommended types of exercise:

- **Aerobic exercise:** Activities like walking, running, swimming, or cycling are ideal for improving mood, as they increase heart rate and stimulate the production of endorphins. Simply walking outdoors, especially in nature, has an additional therapeutic effect by reducing cortisol levels, the stress hormone.
- **Yoga:** Yoga combines physical movement with breathing and relaxation techniques, making it an excellent option for people with depression. It not only improves flexibility and strength but also reduces anxiety and promotes mindfulness, helping people connect with the present moment.
- **Resistance training:** Lifting weights or using resistance bands to strengthen muscles can also be beneficial. This type of exercise has been shown to reduce depression symptoms,

partly because it generates a sense of accomplishment and control over the body, which is particularly helpful for people who feel powerless or out of control in their lives.

- **Group activities:** Participating in team sports or group classes (such as dance or aerobics) not only provides the physical benefits of exercise but also encourages socialization, which can be key to counteracting the isolation that often accompanies depression.

It's essential to start slowly, especially if the person is not used to exercising. The goal is not to perform strenuous activities from the beginning but to create the habit of moving regularly. Even light activities, such as a 20-minute walk a day, can positively impact mood.

9.3. Physical Exercise as Prevention

Exercise is not only useful for treating depression but also for preventing it. People who engage in regular physical activity have a lower risk of developing depression throughout their lives. This is because exercise improves emotional resilience and reduces the risk factors associated with depression, such as chronic stress, social isolation, and self-esteem problems.

How Exercise Acts as Prevention:

- **Stress reduction:** Physical exercise helps release accumulated tension and lowers cortisol levels. Chronic stress is one of the main triggers of depression, so controlling stress through exercise reduces the risk of falling into a depressive state.
- **Improved sleep:** Physical activity regulates sleep cycles, contributing to better-quality rest. Insomnia or sleep problems are both a symptom and a risk factor for depression, so improving sleep through exercise can prevent depressive episodes.
- **Social connection:** As mentioned earlier, participating in sports or exercise groups fosters social interaction, which

helps reduce isolation, another factor that increases the risk of depression.

- **Promoting positive self-esteem:** Feeling physically active and strong, and seeing progress in physical endurance and performance, generates a sense of accomplishment. This positive perception of one's body and abilities is key to preventing depression, as it strengthens self-esteem.

9.4. Case Study: Ana and Her Path to Recovery Through Sports

Ana, a 29-year-old woman, had struggled with depression for much of her adult life. Although she had tried various treatments, such as therapy and antidepressants, she still felt trapped in a cycle of apathy and sadness. Ana had been an active person in her teenage years, but during her years of depression, she had stopped exercising, which worsened her mood and energy levels.

After talking with her therapist, Ana decided to try reintroducing exercise into her daily life, though at first, she wasn't convinced it would help. She started slowly, taking 10- to 15-minute walks around her neighborhood, which helped clear her mind, but without immediate, significant changes.

As the weeks passed, Ana noticed that her energy levels began to improve and that her walks became a routine she looked forward to. She then decided to take it a step further and signed up for a yoga class. Initially, the postures were challenging, but the combination of stretching and conscious breathing provided a calm she hadn't experienced in a long time.

Over time, Ana increased the intensity of her workouts, incorporating longer yoga sessions and alternating them with light jogging in the park. She also joined a beginner's running group, which allowed her to socialize more actively and feel supported by people with similar goals. Simply leaving the house and moving, along with social interaction, gave her a new perspective on her problems.

After several months of maintaining an exercise routine, Ana experienced a significant improvement in her mood. Although she continued with psychological treatment, exercise provided her with an additional tool to manage her depression. Furthermore, the physical routine gave her a sense of control over her life and body, something she had lost during her more difficult years.

Ana's case demonstrates that exercise can play a crucial role in recovering from depression. It not only improves physical symptoms but also acts as a catalyst for emotional well-being and personal motivation.

In this chapter, we explored how physical exercise has a profound impact on treating and preventing depression. From its ability to regulate mood through the release of neurotransmitters to the different types of physical activities recommended for people with depression, it's clear that movement is a powerful tool in the fight against this illness. Through Ana's story, we also saw how sports can help regain control over life and emotional well-being, a key step on the path to recovery.

Chapter 10: The Role of Nutrition in Mental Health

The relationship between nutrition and mental health has garnered increasing attention in recent years. What we eat affects not only our bodies but also our brains, and, consequently, our emotional state. In this chapter, we will explore how nutrition influences depression, the essential nutrients for a healthy brain, and dietary changes that can improve mood. Finally, we will include a practical exercise to create a balanced meal plan that promotes mental health.

10.1. The Relationship Between Nutrition and Depression

More and more studies suggest that there is a direct connection between what we eat and how we feel emotionally. Depression, like many other mental disorders, has a multifactorial basis, with chemical imbalances in the brain playing a key role. Nutrition can influence these imbalances by providing, or lacking, the nutrients necessary for the production of mood-regulating neurotransmitters, such as serotonin, dopamine, and norepinephrine.

When we follow a diet low in essential nutrients, we increase the risk of developing deficiencies that can affect brain function.

Additionally, the excessive consumption of processed foods rich in refined sugars and saturated fats can worsen depressive symptoms. Diets high in these foods are often associated with inflammation in the body and brain, increasing vulnerability to disorders like depression.

On the other hand, a diet rich in whole foods, such as fruits, vegetables, lean proteins, and healthy fats, can protect the brain from oxidative stress and promote optimal mental function. Studies have shown that people who follow healthier dietary patterns, like the Mediterranean diet, are less likely to suffer from depression compared to those who follow more processed Western diets.

10.2. Key Nutrients for a Healthy Brain

For the brain to function optimally and properly regulate mood, it needs several essential nutrients that play important roles in neurotransmitter production and in protecting brain cells. Below are some of the most important nutrients for mental health:

- **Omega-3 Fatty Acids:** These fatty acids, found in fatty fish like salmon, sardines, and tuna, are essential for brain health. Omega-3 helps regulate inflammation and supports communication between brain cells. Various studies have shown that people with low omega-3 levels are more likely to suffer from depression.

- **B Vitamins:** B vitamins, especially B6, B9 (folic acid), and B12, are crucial for the production of neurotransmitters like serotonin and dopamine. Deficiency in these vitamins is associated with an increased risk of depression and mental fatigue. These vitamins can be found in foods like whole grains, legumes, leafy green vegetables, and animal products like eggs and meat.

- **Magnesium:** This mineral helps regulate nervous system functions and is necessary for serotonin production.

Magnesium deficiency can lead to anxiety, fatigue, and depression. Sources of magnesium include nuts, seeds, spinach, and legumes.

- **Vitamin D:** Known as the "sunshine vitamin," vitamin D also plays an important role in mental health. Low levels of vitamin D have been linked to an increased risk of depression. Although sun exposure is the main source of this vitamin, it is also found in foods like fatty fish and eggs, and supplementation may be necessary during winter months.

- **Tryptophan:** Tryptophan is an essential amino acid that the body uses to produce serotonin, the neurotransmitter that regulates mood. This amino acid is found in foods like turkey, chicken, eggs, nuts, and bananas.

- **Zinc:** Zinc is a mineral necessary for immune function and brain health. Zinc deficiency has been linked to a higher likelihood of depression. Zinc-rich foods include beef, pumpkin seeds, chickpeas, and cashews.

10.3. Dietary Changes That Can Help

Making changes to your diet can significantly improve your mood and reduce symptoms of depression. These changes don't need to be drastic; small adjustments can have a big impact over time. Below are some recommendations to improve your diet and support mental health:

- **Increase the consumption of fresh, whole foods:** Prioritize fruits, vegetables, whole grains, and lean proteins over ultra-processed foods. These foods are rich in vitamins, minerals, and antioxidants that protect the brain from oxidative damage and promote better mood.

- **Reduce refined sugars and saturated fats:** Excessive consumption of sugar and unhealthy fats can trigger brain inflammation and negatively affect neurotransmitter production. Try to reduce your intake of sugary drinks, processed pastries, fast food, and processed products.

- **Incorporate more omega-3s:** As mentioned earlier, omega-3 fatty acids are essential for brain health. If you don't eat enough fatty fish, consider adding walnuts, chia seeds, or flaxseeds to your diet, or take an omega-3 supplement.

- **Stay adequately hydrated:** The importance of drinking enough water is often overlooked. Dehydration can lead to fatigue and mental confusion, so it's important to ensure you drink at least eight glasses of water a day.

- **Moderate caffeine intake:** While coffee and tea can have benefits when consumed in moderation, too much caffeine can increase anxiety and nervousness, which can worsen depressive symptoms in some people.

- **Include more fermented foods:** Gut health is closely related to mental health through the gut-brain axis. Fermented foods like yogurt, kefir, sauerkraut, and kimchi contain probiotics that help maintain a healthy gut flora, which can improve mood and reduce inflammation.

10.4. Practical Exercise: Balanced Meal Plan to Improve Mood

This exercise will help you create a weekly meal plan that includes foods rich in essential nutrients to improve your mental health. The key is to ensure your diet is varied and balanced, including foods that promote neurotransmitter production and brain health.

Step 1: Plan Your Main Meals

In a notebook or chart, organize your main meals for the week, ensuring you include sources of lean protein, healthy fats, and plenty of fruits and vegetables. Below is an example of what a weekly plan might look like:

Day	Breakfast	Lunch	Dinner
Monday	Natural yogurt with chia seeds and berries	Spinach salad with chicken, walnuts, avocado	Baked salmon with quinoa and broccoli
Tuesday	Oatmeal with banana and walnuts	Quinoa with roasted vegetables and chickpeas	Grilled chicken with arugula salad
Wednesday	Whole grain toast with avocado and egg	Grilled fish with brown rice and spinach	Vegetable omelet and green salad
Thursday	Spinach, banana, and oatmeal smoothie	Lentil salad with tomatoes and carrots	Roast turkey with potatoes and broccoli
Friday	Scrambled eggs with spinach and mushrooms	Chicken with baked chickpeas and zucchini	Hake with quinoa and spinach salad
Saturday	Cooked oatmeal with almond milk and nuts	Whole wheat pasta with tuna and vegetables	Chickpea salad with tuna and avocado
Sunday	Spinach omelet with tomato and fresh cheese	Roasted chicken with sweet potatoes and coleslaw	Stir-fried tofu with brown rice

Step 2: Include Healthy Snacks

Add healthy snacks between meals, rich in healthy fats and proteins, to keep your energy levels stable throughout the day:

- Fresh fruits like apples, bananas, or oranges
- Nuts or almonds
- Natural yogurt or kefir
- Carrots or cucumber with hummus

Step 3: Adjust and Evaluate

Throughout the week, take note of how you feel physically and emotionally after each meal. Do you feel more energetic or emotionally stable? If you notice improvements, you can continue adjusting your diet to include more of the foods that make you feel good.

This exercise will help you pay more attention to the relationship between what you eat and how you feel, allowing you to create a meal plan that supports both your physical and mental health.

In this chapter, we explored the relationship between nutrition and mental health, highlighting the key nutrients that support a healthy brain and the dietary changes that can help improve depression symptoms. Through the practical meal planning exercise, you will take control of your diet and develop habits that not only promote your physical well-being but also your emotional balance.

Chapter 11: Relationships While Depressed

Depression not only affects the individual experiencing it but also impacts relationships with those closest to them. It is common for depression to lead to social isolation, which can worsen symptoms and make recovery more challenging. In this chapter, we will explore how depression affects personal relationships, strategies for communicating what we are going through, the importance of having a support network, and we will analyze a case study about how Clara, someone facing depression, learned to open up emotionally.

11.1. How Depression Affects Close Relationships

Depression can deeply influence how a person interacts with their loved ones, whether they are family, friends, or romantic partners. Common symptoms like isolation, lack of energy, and irritability often create tension in personal relationships, as the depressed person may have difficulty expressing what they are feeling or may emotionally withdraw.

Some ways in which depression affects relationships include:

- **Isolation:** People with depression tend to avoid social contact. This can be due to fatigue, low self-esteem, or the fear of not being understood. Isolation may make friends and family feel rejected or lead them to misinterpret the behavior, thinking that the depressed person no longer desires their company.

- **Irritability and mood swings:** While we often associate depression with sadness, it can also manifest as irritability. A lack of patience or sudden mood swings can create conflict in close relationships, as those around the person may not understand that this is part of the illness.

- **Emotional disconnection:** One of the most painful characteristics of depression is anhedonia, the inability to feel pleasure in activities that were once enjoyed. This includes a lack of interest in relationships, leading the depressed person to emotionally distance themselves from loved ones.

- **Feelings of guilt:** People with depression often feel guilty about their behavior or feel like a "burden" to others, which reinforces their tendency to isolate themselves. This feeling can intensify if they perceive that their loved ones don't understand what they are going through or if they feel that they are causing tension in their relationships.

11.2. Strategies for Communicating What We Are Going Through

One of the main challenges for people with depression is communicating what they are feeling. Often, the fear of rejection or misunderstanding prevents the person from sharing their experience with close friends or family. However, open communication is essential so that others can offer appropriate support.

Some strategies for communicating what we are going through include:

- **Speaking at the right time:** It's important to find a quiet moment to talk about how you're feeling. Avoiding rushed conversations or speaking in the middle of stressful situations can make it easier to open up emotionally. It might help to say something like, "I need to talk to you about how I've been feeling lately."

- **Explaining depression symptoms:** Depression can be difficult to understand for those who haven't experienced it. Explaining the symptoms and how they affect you can help others understand that behaviors like lack of interest or irritability aren't personal rejections but manifestations of the illness.

- **Using specific examples:** It can be helpful to give specific examples of how you feel or how depression affects your actions. For example, instead of saying, "I feel bad all the time," you might say, "I've noticed I no longer enjoy things I used to, like going for walks or spending time with friends."

- **Asking for support, not solutions:** It's important to clarify that you aren't looking for someone to "fix" you, but rather to accompany you. You can say something like, "I don't need you to tell me what to do, I just need you to listen and be there for me."

- **Being honest about limits:** If you feel exhausted or need space, communicate this clearly. Saying something like, "I don't have the energy to talk much today, but I appreciate you being here" can prevent misunderstandings and frustrations from others.

11.3. The Importance of a Support Network

Having a solid support network is essential for coping with depression. The people we share our emotions with can be a source of relief and comfort. Although they cannot "cure" us, their presence can make a big difference in the recovery process.

- **Company instead of loneliness:** Depression tends to cause isolation, but support from friends and family can help combat this urge. Even if you don't always want to talk, knowing that there are people by your side is reassuring.

- **Emotional support:** Sometimes, just having someone willing to listen without judging or trying to offer solutions can be very beneficial. Knowing that you don't have to face depression alone is a great relief.

- **Practical help:** People in your support network can also offer practical help, like accompanying you to a medical appointment, helping with daily tasks that feel overwhelming, or simply being there during difficult moments.

- **Encouraging self-care:** The people around you can help keep you motivated to maintain healthy habits like exercising, eating well, or attending therapy. Having someone encourage you to take care of yourself can be an important boost when your own motivation is low.

11.4. Case Study: Clara and Her Journey to Open Up Emotionally

Clara, a 33-year-old woman, had been silently dealing with depression for months. She had always been a sociable and cheerful person, but recently her friends and family noticed that she had become more distant. Clara avoided going out, responded with one-word answers, and often canceled plans at the last minute. Her friends thought that maybe she needed space, but in reality, Clara felt trapped in a cycle of sadness and was unable to explain what she was going through.

One day, her best friend, Marta, confronted her: "Clara, I know something is going on. I'm worried about you." At first, Clara tried to deflect the conversation, as she had done before, but Marta's gentle persistence made her feel that she could finally trust someone. Clara explained that she had been feeling empty for months and couldn't find a clear reason for it. "I know it seems like I don't care about anything, but it's just that I don't have the energy for anything," she said through tears.

Marta listened attentively without interrupting. She asked how she could help and, most importantly, made Clara feel that she wasn't alone. From that conversation, Clara felt freer to talk about her depression. She discovered that opening up wasn't as terrifying as she had thought. She also began seeking professional help with Marta's support, who accompanied her to her first therapy session.

Over time, Clara learned that sharing how she felt didn't make her weak but stronger. Although she still had difficult days, her relationship with her family and friends strengthened because they now better understood what she was going through and knew how to support her effectively. The simple act of opening up emotionally was a significant step in her journey toward recovery.

In this chapter, we have seen how depression can affect close relationships and how open communication is key to maintaining support from loved ones. We also explored the importance of a support network for emotional well-being and how the process of opening up, while difficult, can be transformative. Clara's story reminds us that sharing our struggles with others can make a difference, not only in our own lives but also in how those around us support us in difficult times.

Chapter 12: Depression and Work

Depression doesn't just affect our personal lives; it can also have a profound impact on our work life. Facing the workday while dealing with depression can feel overwhelming, as fatigue, lack of concentration, and diminished motivation are common symptoms. In this chapter, we'll discuss the possibility of working while experiencing depression, strategies for maintaining a work-life balance, how to address depression with coworkers or supervisors, and a practical exercise to manage workplace stress when living with depression.

12.1. Is It Possible to Work When We Are Depressed?

Working while depressed can seem like an impossible task for many, as depression affects concentration, motivation, and energy, making it difficult to fulfill job responsibilities. However, many people with depression continue working, and in some cases, work can provide a daily structure that helps maintain a sense of normalcy and stability.

Common challenges of working while depressed:

- **Lack of motivation:** Depression can make even the simplest tasks feel exhausting or meaningless. A person may struggle to find the energy necessary to start or complete their work.

- **Concentration problems:** Staying focused on tasks can become difficult due to mental fatigue, excessive negative thoughts, or feeling emotionally overwhelmed.

- **Physical fatigue:** Many people with depression experience deep fatigue, affecting their ability to keep up with the pace of work.

- **Feelings of guilt or worthlessness:** Depression often generates negative thoughts about oneself, leading a person to feel inadequate or doubt their ability to perform their job, even if they are objectively doing well.

Although working under these conditions is challenging, many people find that work can also provide a temporary distraction from negative thoughts, and a structured work environment can offer a sense of purpose that helps maintain a daily routine. The key is adjusting expectations and seeking support when necessary.

12.2. Strategies for Maintaining a Work-Life Balance

Finding a balance between work and depression requires strategies that allow you to manage symptoms without neglecting professional responsibilities. Here are some ideas that can help you maintain a healthy balance:

- **Break work into smaller tasks:** Instead of feeling overwhelmed by large projects or long deadlines, break tasks into smaller, manageable steps. Completing small actions can create a sense of accomplishment and prevent you from feeling swamped.

- **Planning and prioritization:** Use a daily task list and focus on the most important items. This will help you stay organized and maintain concentration. You can also prioritize more complex tasks during times of the day when you have more energy.

- **Take regular breaks:** Schedule short breaks every 60 or 90 minutes to recharge and maintain focus. Standing up, walking around, or deep breathing for a few minutes can relieve tension and improve your concentration.

- **Set clear boundaries:** If you're working from home or in a demanding environment, it's important to set boundaries to avoid burnout. Learning to say "no" or delegating tasks when necessary can prevent work overload, which could worsen depression.

- **Practice self-compassion:** Depression generates self-critical thoughts that can make you feel useless or guilty for not performing at your best. It's essential to remember that you are dealing with an illness, and your productivity may be temporarily affected. Allow yourself to make mistakes and avoid comparing yourself to others.

12.3. How to Address Depression with Coworkers or Supervisors

Talking about depression in the workplace can be a sensitive topic, and deciding when and how to share what you're going through depends on each situation. However, in some cases, sharing your experience may be necessary to receive support or to temporarily adjust your responsibilities. Here are some guidelines for addressing the conversation with coworkers or supervisors:

- **Consider whether it's necessary to share:** It's not always necessary to share your diagnosis with coworkers or bosses. Assess whether depression is significantly interfering with your job performance. If you believe you need adjustments in your responsibilities, it might be helpful to inform your supervisor or HR department.

- **Choose who and when to tell:** If you decide to talk about your depression, carefully choose someone you feel comfortable with. It could be a trusted coworker, your direct boss, or someone from HR. Plan the conversation at a quiet time with no interruptions.

- **Be honest and direct, but without too many details:** You don't need to share every personal detail. What's important is to communicate how depression is affecting you and what type of support or adjustments you might need. You can say something like, "I'm going through a personal situation that is affecting my energy and concentration. I'm working on it, but I may need some temporary adjustments to better manage my workload."

- **Request reasonable adjustments:** If your depression is severely interfering with your ability to work, you could request temporary adjustments to your schedule or assigned tasks. This could include working from home, reducing work hours, or delegating some more demanding tasks while you recover.

- **Be prepared for questions:** Your supervisor or coworkers may have questions about what you're experiencing. Decide beforehand how much information you want to share. In some cases, it may be helpful to provide a medical report if you are requesting job adjustments.

12.4. Practical Exercise: Managing Work Stress and Depression

To help you manage work stress while coping with depression, we propose a practical exercise that will allow you to identify stressors in your job and create a plan to handle them more effectively.

Step 1: Identify work stressors
Make a list of the situations or tasks at work that stress you out or that are difficult to handle due to depression. These could include tight deadlines, long meetings, tedious tasks, or feeling overwhelmed.

Example:

- Complex tasks with tight deadlines

- Long and exhausting meetings

- Lack of concentration when writing reports

Step 2: Identify resources and strategies
For each stressor, identify a resource or strategy you can implement to reduce its impact. This could include talking to your boss, reorganizing your schedule, asking for help from a coworker, or using relaxation techniques during the day.

Example:

- Complex tasks with tight deadlines: Break tasks into smaller parts and set mini-deadlines for each. Talk to your boss about adjusting deadlines if necessary.

- Long and exhausting meetings: Propose shorter meetings or request to participate only in the most relevant parts. Take breaks before and after the meeting.

- Lack of concentration when writing reports: Work in short blocks of time (20-30 minutes) with breaks to clear your mind.

Step 3: Incorporate self-care techniques

Throughout the workday, it's important to incorporate breaks for self-care. Identify times in your day when you can practice some relaxation or rest technique. Here are some ideas:

- Practice deep breathing or mindful meditation for 5 minutes before a meeting.

- Take a short walk during lunch to clear your mind.

- Use progressive muscle relaxation to relieve physical tension while sitting at your desk.

Step 4: Weekly review

At the end of the week, review how you felt with the strategies you implemented. Did they help reduce stress? What can you adjust for the following week? Keeping a log will help you identify which methods are most effective for you.

This chapter has explored how depression can affect job performance but has also offered useful strategies for balancing work with emotional well-being. From learning to manage stress and breaking tasks down to the importance of communicating what you are experiencing with coworkers or supervisors, working while dealing with depression is possible with the right adjustments. Through the practical exercise provided, you can learn to better handle work stress and protect your mental health in the long term.

Chapter 13: Depression in Adolescents

Adolescent depression is a growing issue that often goes unnoticed. While the symptoms may be similar to those in adults, adolescents face unique challenges due to their stage of emotional and social development. In this chapter, we will explore the differences between depression in adolescents and adults, the warning signs to watch for, and how parents and educators can help. Finally, we will discuss the case of Luis, a teenager who didn't know how to ask for help.

13.1. Differences Between Depression in Adults and Adolescents

Depression affects both adults and adolescents, but it manifests differently in teens due to specific emotional, hormonal, and social factors related to adolescence. Here are some key differences:

- **Mood swings versus stable symptoms:** Adolescents often experience more extreme or volatile mood swings. While adults tend to have persistent sadness, adolescents may alternate between episodes of irritability, frustration, anger, and sadness. These mood changes are often mistaken for "typical" teenage behavior, making it harder to recognize depression.

- **Social isolation:** Adults with depression tend to withdraw from their social and family environments, but in adolescents, isolation can manifest more subtly, such as avoiding activities they once enjoyed, ceasing to spend time with friends, or emotionally distancing themselves from family. Teens might also spend more time alone in their rooms or avoid any form of interaction.

- **Academic decline:** While adults may experience work-related difficulties, adolescents often show a drop in academic performance, lose interest in their studies, or even skip classes. Lack of concentration and fatigue contribute to this problem, and many teens can't explain why they feel so disconnected from their schoolwork.

- **Risky behavior:** A specific aspect of depression in adolescents is an increase in impulsive or risky behaviors, which can include drug or alcohol use, reckless driving, or engaging in self-destructive acts. These behaviors may be attempts to escape their emotions or seek attention from adults.

- **Feelings of misunderstanding:** Adolescents often feel that adults don't understand their emotional world, leading to a lack of communication and increased emotional distance. They may feel that they have no one to turn to, further deepening their isolation and exacerbating their depression.

13.2. Warning Signs in Adolescents

Because depression in adolescents can be mistaken for the typical ups and downs of this stage of life, it is essential to be aware of warning signs that indicate a more profound problem. Some of the most common signs include:

- **Sudden mood changes:** Frequent irritability, sadness, or anger that seems disproportionate or constant.

- **Social isolation:** Avoiding time with friends or family and preferring to be alone more frequently than usual.

- **Changes in sleep and eating habits:** Sleeping too much or too little, along with changes in appetite—either overeating or eating very little.

- **Loss of interest in activities:** No longer enjoying activities they once liked, such as sports, music, or hobbies.

- **Poor academic performance:** Declining grades, disinterest in school, trouble concentrating, and unexplained absences.

- **Frequent physical complaints:** Headaches, digestive issues, or muscle pains without a physical cause, which can be physical manifestations of emotional distress.

- **Self-destructive behaviors:** Any sign of self-harm, such as cutting, or comments about death or suicide, require immediate attention.

13.3. How Parents and Educators Can Help

Adolescents with depression need support from trusted adults in their lives, but they often don't know how to ask for help or feel embarrassed to do so. Parents, educators, and other close adults can play a crucial role in detecting signs of depression and providing effective support. Here are some ways to help:

- **Encourage open communication:** Often, teenagers feel that their parents or teachers don't listen to or understand them. It is important for adults to create an environment where the adolescent feels safe to talk about their feelings without fear of being judged or dismissed. Asking how they feel without pressuring them and showing empathy is key to opening channels of communication.

- **Listen without judgment:** If a teenager is willing to talk about their emotional state, adults should avoid responses that minimize the problem, such as "It's just a phase" or "You need to think positively." Instead, it's crucial to listen attentively, validate their emotions, and refrain from offering unsolicited advice.

- **Establish a structured routine:** Adolescents with depression often feel overwhelmed by responsibilities or lose control of their daily routine. Parents can help create a balanced routine that includes time for study, rest, physical activity, and leisure, always considering the teenager's abilities and needs.

- **Seek professional help:** If you suspect a teenager is depressed, it's essential to seek professional help as soon as possible. A psychologist or psychiatrist can provide the proper diagnosis and offer treatment, whether through individual therapy, family therapy, or, in some cases, medication.

- **Model healthy behavior:** Adolescents observe and learn from the adults in their lives. Demonstrating healthy self-care habits, such as stress management, exercise, and emotional openness, can help them develop tools to manage their own emotions.

- **Collaborate with the educational environment:** Educators can be valuable allies for parents in identifying mental health issues. Maintaining open communication with teachers can help monitor the adolescent's academic performance and implement accommodations if needed.

13.4. Case Study: Luis, a Teenager Who Didn't Know How to Ask for Help

Luis was 15 years old and had always been a committed and cheerful student, but in recent months, his attitude had changed. He started missing classes, and his grades dropped dramatically. He spent a lot of time alone in his room, avoiding both family and friends. Although he used to be sociable, he stopped attending sports activities and avoided any type of social gathering. His parents thought it was just a phase, but they became more concerned when they found out Luis had been crying alone in his room for no apparent reason.

Luis felt an overwhelming sadness but didn't know how to explain it. He didn't understand why he felt so bad, and the idea of telling someone about it seemed humiliating. He believed that no one would understand, or they would tell him, "It will pass." However, his mother, concerned about the changes she saw, decided to address the situation.

One day, she sat down to talk with him, not to interrogate him but to listen. She said, "Luis, I've noticed you seem sadder lately and that you've stopped doing things you used to enjoy. You don't have to talk now, but I want you to know I'm here whenever you need me, and what you're feeling is important." Luis didn't respond immediately, but knowing his mother was willing to listen without judgment gave him a sense of relief.

A few days later, when Luis felt more comfortable, he confided in his mother about how bad he had been feeling and that he didn't know why he was so sad. Together, they sought help from a psychologist, where Luis began to understand his depression and work on strategies to improve his mood. The support from his family and early intervention prevented his depression from worsening.

Luis's case shows how compassionate parental support, open communication, and seeking professional help can be crucial for a teenager who doesn't know how to ask for help.

In this chapter, we have explored the differences between depression in adolescents and adults, the warning signs parents and educators should watch for, and ways adults can provide emotional and practical support. Luis's story illustrates the importance of creating a safe space for teenagers to feel capable of talking about their emotions and seeking help when they need it. Understanding depression in young people and acting early is vital for their well-being and emotional development.

Chapter 14: Depression in Older Adults

Depression in older adults is often an underestimated reality. Frequently, depressive symptoms in the elderly are mistaken for the effects of aging or physical illnesses, which can lead to depression being undiagnosed or inadequately treated. This chapter examines the specific challenges of depression in older adults, how to detect it in this stage of life, intervention strategies, and presents the case of Pedro, a retiree who struggled with depression.

14.1. The Challenge of Depression in Old Age

Depression in older adults presents a unique challenge due to the multiple factors that interact during this stage of life. Often, depression in old age is overlooked or considered a "normal" part of aging, when in reality it is a disorder that requires attention and treatment.

Some of the main factors contributing to depression in old age include:

- **Loss of loved ones:** The death of spouses, friends, or close family members can trigger deep grief that, if not properly managed, can turn into depression.

- **Social isolation:** As people age, they tend to have fewer opportunities for social interaction, which can lead to feelings of loneliness. Retirement, lack of mobility, or the loss of friendships also contribute to this isolation.

- **Physical health problems:** Chronic illnesses such as arthritis, cancer, diabetes, or hypertension are common in old age and can lead to feelings of helplessness or hopelessness. Additionally, some physical illnesses can cause chronic pain, which exacerbates depression.

- **Dependence and loss of autonomy:** As older adults face physical or cognitive limitations, they may experience a loss of control over their lives. Dependence on others for daily activities can generate feelings of frustration, shame, or worthlessness.

- **Changes in social roles:** Retirement, though anticipated, often leads to a loss of identity and purpose. People who have defined themselves through their work may struggle to find a new sense of usefulness.

These factors create an environment prone to the development of depression, and it is important to address them proactively to ensure the mental well-being of older adults.

14.2. How to Detect Depression in Older Adults

Detecting depression in older adults can be difficult because the symptoms are often confused with signs of aging or other physical health problems. Additionally, older adults tend not to express their emotions in the same way younger people do, which may lead them to hide or minimize their emotional distress.

Some warning signs to watch for include:

- **Loss of interest in daily activities:** If an older person stops showing interest in activities they used to enjoy, such as hobbies, visiting family, or going for walks, it could be a sign of depression.

- **Changes in appetite or sleep:** Depression in older adults can manifest through insomnia, excessive sleep, or significant changes in appetite. This may lead to unexplained weight loss or gain.

- **Constant fatigue:** A lack of energy or extreme tiredness not related to specific physical problems can be a sign of depression.

- **Cognitive problems:** Older adults with depression may have trouble concentrating, making decisions, or remembering things. Sometimes, depression in older adults is mistakenly diagnosed as dementia because of these cognitive issues.

- **Irritability or mood changes:** Although sadness is a classic symptom of depression, in older adults, depression often appears as irritability, impatience, or constant frustration.

- **Social withdrawal:** If an older person withdraws from their social life or avoids contact with friends and family, they may be experiencing depression.

- **Frequent physical complaints:** Older adults with depression often complain of physical symptoms such as headaches, digestive problems, or body aches that do not have an identifiable medical cause.

It is important to remember that depression in old age can present more subtly and that physical complaints may be a sign of emotional distress that is not directly expressed.

14.3. Intervention Strategies in Old Age

Intervening in cases of depression in older adults requires a careful approach tailored to the needs of this stage of life. Below are some strategies that can be effective in improving mental well-being in older adults:

- **Psychological therapy:** Therapies such as Cognitive Behavioral Therapy (CBT) have proven effective in treating depression in older adults. CBT helps people identify negative thoughts and develop new ways to cope with the emotional and physical challenges of aging.

- **Reminiscence therapy:** This therapy involves reviewing and reflecting on past experiences, helping older adults find meaning in their lives and connect with positive memories. It can be useful in improving self-esteem and reducing feelings of worthlessness.

- **Adapted physical activity:** Regular exercise, adapted to the person's physical capabilities, can be a powerful tool for combating depression. Activities such as walking, swimming, or gentle exercises help improve mood by releasing endorphins and keeping the body active, which is essential for both physical and mental health.

- **Fostering social connections:** Keeping older adults connected with their family, friends, or community groups is essential in preventing isolation. Encouraging participation in social activities such as book clubs, craft classes, or family gatherings can help reduce loneliness.

- **Antidepressant medications:** In some cases, antidepressants may be necessary, especially if therapy alone is not enough to manage the symptoms of depression. It is important that medications are prescribed and monitored by a medical professional, as older adults may have particular sensitivities to certain drugs or be taking other medications that could interact.

- **Structured routine:** Maintaining a daily routine helps provide structure and meaning to older adults' lives, which is especially important if they feel purposeless after retirement. Including planned activities, from household chores to leisure time, can help prevent boredom and negative thoughts.

14.4. Case Study: Pedro, a Retiree Struggling with Depression

Pedro, 70 years old, had been retired for a few years after working his entire life as a schoolteacher. At first, he enjoyed his free time, but over the years, he began to feel increasingly lonely and purposeless. His wife had passed away, and his children lived far away. Pedro went from being an active and engaged person to someone who avoided leaving the house, slept most of the day, and no longer found pleasure in activities he used to enjoy, such as gardening or reading history books.

His friends noticed that he had stopped attending the weekly meetings, and when they called him, he always found an excuse not to go out. He often complained of aches and pains, but when he went to the doctor, no clear physical cause was found. His children, worried, visited him and noticed how much he had changed. They decided to accompany him to an appointment with a psychologist specializing in older adults.

During therapy, Pedro confessed that he felt "useless" and couldn't find a reason to get up in the morning. The lack of social interaction, the loss of his wife, and retirement had contributed to a deep sense of emptiness. The psychologist worked with Pedro through Cognitive Behavioral Therapy (CBT) sessions to help him identify these negative thoughts and find new ways to give his life meaning. He was encouraged to join a local book club, something he had always enjoyed in the past, and to take up gardening again, even on a small scale.

Over time, Pedro began to notice small improvements. He started going out more often, connected with people his age in the book club, and discovered that he had something to look forward to each week. Although the depression didn't completely disappear, Pedro learned to manage it better and, most importantly, began to feel that his life had meaning again.

This case shows how, with the right support, older adults can overcome depression and regain the motivation to participate actively in life.

In this chapter, we have examined depression in older adults, a reality that is often overlooked. From the specific difficulties of this stage to the importance of detection and intervention strategies, it is essential that older adults receive the necessary support to effectively address depression. Through Pedro's case, we have seen how appropriate intervention, family support, and reconnection with meaningful activities can help improve emotional well-being in old age.

Chapter 15: Postpartum Depression

Postpartum depression is a disorder that affects many women after the birth of their baby. This period, often anticipated as one of the happiest in a woman's life, can be clouded by feelings of sadness, exhaustion, and hopelessness. While it's common to experience the "baby blues" (mild emotional fluctuations) in the days following childbirth, postpartum depression is more severe and can last much longer if untreated. In this chapter, we will explore what postpartum depression is, its risk factors, how to detect it, the most effective treatments, and a case study of Marta, who overcame depression after the birth of her child.

15.1. Understanding Postpartum Depression

Postpartum depression is a type of depression that affects women after giving birth. While many mothers experience brief periods of sadness or anxiety known as the "baby blues," which are normal and last only a few days, postpartum depression is more serious and persistent. It can start in the weeks following childbirth or even months later, and without proper treatment, it can last for years.

Postpartum depression is not a sign of weakness or failure as a mother. It is a disorder with biological, psychological, and social causes and requires treatment. Women with postpartum depression may experience a variety of symptoms, including:

- Deep feelings of sadness or emptiness

- Lack of interest or pleasure in daily life, including in their relationship with the baby

- Extreme fatigue or lack of energy

- Trouble sleeping (even when the baby is sleeping)

- Intense anxiety or panic attacks

- Feelings of guilt, worthlessness, or shame

- Difficulty concentrating or making decisions

- Thoughts of harming themselves or the baby (in severe cases)

It is important to note that postpartum depression does not only affect first-time mothers; it can occur after any pregnancy. Additionally, while it is more common in women, men can also experience symptoms of postpartum depression due to changes in family dynamics, stress, and lack of sleep.

15.2. Risk Factors and How to Detect It

Postpartum depression can affect any mother, but certain risk factors increase the likelihood of developing this disorder. Detecting it early is crucial to start treatment and prevent it from worsening or lasting longer.

Risk factors:

- **History of depression or anxiety:** Women who have experienced depression, anxiety, or mood disorders before or during pregnancy are at higher risk of developing postpartum depression.

- **Hormonal changes:** After childbirth, hormone levels like estrogen and progesterone drop sharply, which can trigger emotional changes and affect the brain's chemical balance.

- **Stress and lack of support:** Mothers who lack an emotional or practical support system may feel overwhelmed by the responsibilities of caring for a newborn.

- **Complications during childbirth or baby care:** Mothers who have had difficult deliveries, medical complications, or whose babies are born prematurely or with health issues are more likely to suffer from postpartum depression.

- **Breastfeeding difficulties:** Social pressure and expectations about breastfeeding can be a source of stress and frustration, especially if women encounter difficulties.

- **Socioeconomic factors:** Economic difficulties, lack of resources, or employment concerns can also increase the risk of postpartum depression.

How to detect it:

- **Duration and intensity:** If feelings of sadness, anxiety, or hopelessness persist beyond the first two weeks after birth or are very intense, it is important to consult a professional. The difference between the "baby blues" and postpartum depression lies in the duration and severity of the symptoms.

- **Difficulty bonding with the baby:** Mothers who feel unable to emotionally connect with their baby or who don't experience the expected pleasure or joy when interacting with them could be suffering from postpartum depression.

- **Feeling extremely overwhelmed:** If daily tasks, such as caring for the baby or meeting basic family needs, seem impossible to manage, it could be a sign of depression.

15.3. Effective Treatments for Postpartum Depression

The good news is that postpartum depression is treatable, and there are several intervention options that can help mothers regain their emotional well-being. Treatment options include:

- **Psychological therapy:** Cognitive Behavioral Therapy (CBT) and interpersonal therapy have been shown to be effective in treating postpartum depression. These therapies help women identify and change negative thoughts, manage anxiety, and improve their relationship with the baby and family environment.

- **Support groups:** Support groups for mothers with postpartum depression can be an excellent way to share experiences, receive practical advice, and feel understood by other women going through the same thing. Both in-person and online groups can provide a valuable support network.

- **Antidepressant medication:** In some cases, antidepressants may be necessary, especially if symptoms are severe or do not improve with therapy alone. Doctors can prescribe antidepressants that are safe to use during breastfeeding, such as selective serotonin reuptake inhibitors (SSRIs), which help restore chemical balance in the brain.

- **Family support:** The involvement of a partner, family members, and close friends is essential. Often, mothers with postpartum depression need help with daily tasks, from caring for the baby to grocery shopping or cleaning. Additionally, close emotional support can make the mother feel less alone in her struggle.

- **Self-care:** Mothers often feel guilty about taking time for themselves, but self-care is essential for recovery. Getting enough sleep (when possible), eating well, and finding moments for rest or recreation can make a big difference in improving mood.

15.4. Case Study: Marta and Overcoming Depression After Her Child's Birth

Marta, 32, had eagerly awaited the birth of her first child. She had an uncomplicated pregnancy, and although she was nervous about the delivery, she had no history of mental health issues. However, after giving birth to her son, she began to feel different. Instead of the joy she had anticipated, she felt overwhelmed, sad, and extremely fatigued.

During the first few weeks, Marta attributed her feelings to lack of sleep and the stress of being a first-time mother. However, as weeks turned into months, Marta realized that something was wrong. She couldn't enjoy her baby, felt disconnected from her husband, and started having disturbing thoughts, such as believing her baby would be better off without her.

Her husband noticed the change in Marta and encouraged her to talk to her doctor. Though hesitant at first, Marta decided to seek help and was referred to a psychologist specializing in postpartum depression. In therapy, Marta learned that what she was experiencing was not unusual and that there was treatment to help her overcome it. She began attending Cognitive Behavioral Therapy (CBT) sessions, where she worked on changing her negative thoughts and learned to manage the anxiety that motherhood was causing her.

Additionally, Marta joined a local support group for mothers with postpartum depression, which allowed her to share her experience with other women going through the same thing. Over time, her symptoms began to improve. She also accepted help from her family, who took turns caring for the baby for a few hours each day, allowing her to rest and recover.

After six months, Marta felt she had regained control of her life. She had learned to enjoy motherhood, felt more connected to her baby and partner, and was grateful she had sought help when she needed it.

Marta's case illustrates how, with the right support and treatment, it is possible to overcome postpartum depression and reconnect with the baby and family in a healthy way.

Chapter 16: Depression and Trauma

Trauma is one of the most frequent underlying causes of depression, as it can leave deep emotional scars that affect mental well-being in the long term. Trauma can trigger depression at any stage of life, and it is often not fully recognized or addressed, which perpetuates depressive symptoms. In this chapter, we will explore the relationship between trauma and depression, the most effective therapies to treat trauma, how trauma changes the brain, and a practical exercise to confront trauma with compassion.

16.1. The Relationship Between Trauma and Depression

Trauma, whether caused by a single overwhelming event (such as an accident, assault, or natural disaster) or by prolonged experiences (such as childhood abuse, domestic violence, or emotional neglect), has a profound impact on the psyche. Many people who experience trauma develop depression as a result of unprocessed pain, persistent fear, and emotional changes that arise after the traumatic experience.

Depression can emerge after trauma due to several factors:

- **Feelings of helplessness or hopelessness:** People who have suffered trauma often feel trapped in their pain, with a sense that they have no control over their lives or emotions. These feelings can generate a deep state of hopelessness, one of the core components of depression.

- **Guilt or shame:** Those who have experienced trauma, especially abuse, often blame themselves for what happened, even when they bear no responsibility. This sense of guilt can fuel low self-esteem and constant self-criticism, which in turn fuel depression.

- **Persistent anxiety:** After trauma, many people live in a state of hypervigilance, expecting something bad to happen at any moment. This constant anxiety can emotionally and physically exhaust a person, increasing the risk of developing depression.

- **Flashbacks and reliving the trauma:** People who have experienced trauma may relive it repeatedly, either through flashbacks or intrusive thoughts. This cycle of re-experiencing can lead to avoiding certain situations or people, which often results in social isolation and, subsequently, depression.

The effects of trauma do not disappear on their own. If not properly addressed, they can remain dormant for years, contributing to depression and affecting daily life in profound and painful ways.

16.2. Therapies for Treating Underlying Trauma

There are several treatment methods available to address the underlying trauma that may be contributing to depression. Below are some of the most effective therapies:

- **Trauma-Focused Cognitive Behavioral Therapy (CBT):** CBT helps individuals identify negative thoughts associated with trauma and replace them with more balanced and realistic thoughts. It also includes gradual exposure to traumatic memories or situations, allowing the person to process the trauma without feeling overwhelmed.

- **Prolonged Exposure Therapy:** This type of therapy involves confronting, in a controlled and safe manner, the memories and emotions associated with the trauma. Through repeated exposure, individuals can begin to reduce their fear and avoid the intense emotional response that comes with recalling the trauma.

- **EMDR (Eye Movement Desensitization and Reprocessing):** EMDR is a therapy based on processing traumatic memories through bilateral stimulation (such as eye movements), which helps the brain process the trauma differently. It is particularly effective for people suffering from post-traumatic stress disorder (PTSD) and can help reduce depression symptoms associated with trauma.

- **Compassion-Focused Therapy:** This therapy focuses on teaching individuals to treat themselves with kindness and understanding. Many people who have experienced trauma harshly criticize themselves for their emotional responses or inability to "move on" from the pain. Compassion-focused therapy helps them develop a healthier, gentler relationship with themselves.

- **Acceptance and Commitment Therapy (ACT):** Instead of focusing solely on changing thoughts, ACT helps individuals accept their emotions and traumatic experiences while committing to actions aligned with their values. This therapy can be useful in helping people stop fighting against emotional pain and instead learn to live fully with their emotions.

- **Somatic Therapy:** Since trauma affects not only the mind but also the body, somatic therapy focuses on releasing physical and emotional tension trapped in the body. It uses techniques such as deep breathing, movement, and body awareness to help individuals process trauma on both a physical and emotional level.

16.3. How Trauma Changes the Brain

Trauma has a significant impact on the brain, affecting how people process emotions and respond to stress. Some of the most common changes include:

- **Hypervigilance:** Trauma affects the amygdala, the part of the brain responsible for emotional responses and processing fear. In people who have experienced trauma, the amygdala can become hyperactive, leading to a constant state of alertness or hypervigilance, where the person is always expecting something bad to happen.

- **Problems in the hippocampus:** The hippocampus is the region of the brain associated with memory and emotional regulation. After trauma, the hippocampus can shrink, making it difficult to process traumatic memories. This can cause traumatic memories to remain "stuck," replaying over and over instead of being processed and properly stored.

- **Alterations in the prefrontal cortex:** This region of the brain is responsible for decision-making and emotional regulation. After trauma, the prefrontal cortex can become less active, making it harder to regulate intense emotions or make clear decisions, contributing to symptoms of depression and anxiety.

Trauma not only affects how a person thinks or feels but literally alters the brain's structure. These changes can increase the likelihood of developing depression, PTSD, and other mental disorders. However, neuroplasticity, the brain's ability to adapt and change, means that with proper treatment, these effects can be reversed or at least diminished over time.

16.4. Practical Exercise: Facing Trauma with Compassion

The following exercise is designed to help you begin addressing your trauma from a perspective of compassion and self-care. Instead of blaming yourself or avoiding your emotions, this exercise will help you acknowledge the pain of your trauma and treat yourself with the understanding and kindness you deserve.

Step 1: Find a safe space

Choose a quiet place where you feel safe and comfortable. Sit in a relaxed position and begin with a few deep breaths to calm your mind and body.

Step 2: Acknowledge the pain

Think about the trauma you have experienced, but don't force yourself to relive all the details. Instead, simply acknowledge how this trauma has affected your emotional and physical life. You can say aloud or in your mind: "I know I have been through something painful, and it has affected me deeply."

Step 3: Bring compassion to yourself

Imagine that someone you love deeply is going through what you have gone through. How would you speak to them? What words of comfort would you offer? Now, take those same words and offer them to yourself. Say phrases like: "It makes sense that I feel this way after what I have been through," or "I'm doing the best I can to overcome this pain."

Step 4: Develop a supportive image

Close your eyes and visualize a person, figure, or even a part of yourself that represents compassion. It could be a loved one, a spiritual figure, or a symbol that comforts you. Imagine this figure offering you support, reminding you that you are not alone and that healing is possible over time.

Step 5: Accept what you feel

Accept any emotion that arises during this exercise, without judging it or trying to change it. If you feel sadness, fear, or anger, give yourself permission to feel those emotions without pressuring yourself to "get over them" quickly. Repeat in your mind: "It's okay to feel what I'm feeling."

Step 6: Practice daily

This exercise is most effective when practiced regularly. Try to spend a few minutes each day offering yourself these words of compassion and reconnecting with the supportive image you've created. Over time, you will develop greater capacity to face trauma with kindness and without guilt.

In this chapter, we have explored the profound relationship between trauma and depression, showing how traumatic experiences affect both the mind and body. We reviewed effective therapies for treating trauma, the changes trauma causes in the brain, and a practical exercise to face emotional pain with compassion. Facing trauma is not easy, but with the right treatment and a compassionate attitude toward yourself, it is possible to begin the journey toward healing and the recovery of mental well-being.

Chapter 17: Preventing Relapses

One of the main concerns for individuals who have overcome depression is the possibility of a relapse. Depression is a chronic and recurrent disorder for many people, which means that even after improvement, there is always a risk of symptoms returning. However, there are steps that can be taken to minimize this risk and maintain good mental health over the long term. In this chapter, we will explore how to detect early warning signs, strategies to maintain emotional well-being, the importance of continuing preventive treatment, and a practical exercise to create a personalized relapse prevention plan.

17.1. How to Detect Early Warning Signs

One key to preventing a depression relapse is learning to recognize early warning signs. These signs can vary from person to person, but it is important to be aware of changes in mood, behavior, or energy levels that may indicate the symptoms are returning.

Some common early warning signs include:

- **Changes in sleep:** Insomnia or excessive sleep are often early signs that depression may be returning. If you notice that you are sleeping more or less than usual without a clear reason, it's important to pay attention to this change.

- **Lack of energy:** Feeling extreme fatigue, lack of motivation, or physical exhaustion that doesn't improve with rest can be a warning sign. If you start to feel that daily tasks are becoming overwhelming again, it may be time to take action.

- **Loss of interest in activities:** If you begin losing interest in activities you once enjoyed, such as socializing with friends, playing sports, or engaging in hobbies, this change may be a sign that depression is reappearing.

- **Social isolation:** Withdrawing from the people who matter to you and avoiding social interaction is a red flag. Isolation can perpetuate depression symptoms, so it's crucial to recognize when you're starting to distance yourself from others.

- **Negative thoughts or self-criticism:** Depression often accompanies recurrent negative thoughts, such as feeling unworthy or incapable of handling challenges. If you notice these thoughts reemerging, it's essential to take immediate action.

- **Changes in appetite:** Eating significantly more or less than usual can be an early warning sign of a depression relapse.

Monitoring these signals will help you identify when something is wrong and when it's time to seek help or adjust your coping strategies before symptoms worsen.

17.2. Strategies for Long-Term Mental Health

Maintaining mental health after overcoming a depressive episode requires ongoing effort. Below are some effective strategies to preserve emotional well-being in the long term:

- **Maintain a routine:** Daily routines provide a sense of structure and control. Having set times for sleep, meals, and exercise can help maintain emotional balance. Planning time for self-care is also important, whether for reading, meditating, or practicing a hobby.

- **Regular exercise:** Physical activity has positive effects on mood by releasing endorphins, known as the "happiness hormones." Incorporating activities such as walking, swimming, cycling, or yoga can help reduce stress and improve emotional well-being.

- **Healthy eating:** Following a balanced diet rich in nutrients that support mental health (such as omega-3 fatty acids, B vitamins, and antioxidants) is key to long-term well-being. Avoid excessive refined sugars and ultra-processed foods that can affect your energy and mood.

- **Mindfulness and meditation:** Mindfulness is a valuable tool for staying connected to the present and managing stress. Practicing mindfulness or meditation regularly can help you observe your emotions without being overwhelmed by them, reducing the risk of relapses.

- **Ongoing therapy:** Even if you feel better, continuing therapy can be beneficial for maintaining emotional balance. Regular sessions with a therapist can help monitor your progress and adjust strategies to prevent the return of symptoms.

- **Support network:** Maintaining a strong support network is essential. Surrounding yourself with people who understand you and offer emotional support can make a difference. Don't hesitate to reach out to friends, family, or support groups if you feel the need to talk or share your concerns.

- **Fostering emotional self-care:** Engage in activities that help you recharge emotionally. This can include creative activities like writing or painting, or simply enjoying quiet moments for yourself. The key is to include these activities in your routine as a form of prevention.

17.3. The Importance of Continuing Preventive Treatment

Once depression symptoms have improved, it's common to think that treatment is no longer needed. However, continuing with preventive treatment is crucial to avoiding relapses. Many people experience significant improvement with medications, therapy, or a combination of both, but stopping treatment too soon can increase the risk of a relapse.

Here are some reasons why continuing preventive treatment is important:

- **Consolidating improvement:** Even if you feel better, your brain may still be in the recovery process. Continuing medication or therapy helps stabilize positive changes and prevent symptoms from reappearing.

- **Strengthening coping strategies:** Therapy helps develop and reinforce strategies to cope with emotional challenges. Maintaining sessions, even if less frequent, can help keep these skills active.

- **Avoiding rebound effects:** Stopping antidepressants or discontinuing therapy abruptly can cause symptoms to return quickly. It's important to follow your doctor or therapist's recommendations and, in the case of medications, gradually reduce the dose if it's considered no longer necessary.

- **Managing difficult situations:** Life always presents challenges, and continuing treatment prepares you to face them in a healthier way. Even if you feel well, maintaining professional support helps you be better prepared for stressful situations.

17.4. Practical Exercise: Creating a Relapse Prevention Plan

This exercise will help you create a personalized relapse prevention plan, based on your experiences and needs. The goal of this plan is to serve as a guide to maintain emotional well-being and act quickly if you notice warning signs.

Step 1: Identify your personal warning signs
Reflect on the signs you noticed before your depression worsened in

the past. These signs may include changes in mood, behavior, sleep, or energy. Make a list of the most common signs for you.

Example:

- Difficulty concentrating
- Feeling like I don't want to see anyone
- Sleeping more than usual or not being able to sleep
- Overeating or losing appetite

Step 2: Identify your triggers
Make a list of the factors that tend to trigger episodes of depression in your case. These may include stress, traumatic events, social isolation, or major life changes.

Example:

- Work or study stress
- Family or relationship conflicts
- Drastic changes in daily routine
- Prolonged loneliness

Step 3: Develop coping strategies
Write down strategies that have worked for you in the past or new ideas to manage triggers and warning signs. Include both practical and emotional techniques.

Example:

- Exercise for at least 30 minutes a day
- Call a close friend when I feel isolated
- Take a 5-minute deep breathing break during stressful moments
- Attend therapy sessions once a month as a preventive measure

Step 4: Create a support network
List the people you can turn to if you feel symptoms returning.
Include friends, family, and healthcare professionals.

Example:

- My partner, available to talk when I need it

- My therapist, regular sessions every two weeks

- My online mental health support group

- A close friend I feel comfortable sharing with

Step 5: Establish an action plan
Define the actions you will take if you detect an imminent relapse.
Be clear and specific about the steps you'll follow.

Example:

- If I notice warning signs, I will talk to my therapist
  immediately.

- I will increase the time dedicated to self-care, such as
  meditation or exercise, in my daily routine.

- I will inform my partner or a close friend about how I'm
  feeling so they are aware.

- I will review with my doctor the possibility of adjusting
  medication if symptoms persist.

Step 6: Review and adjust the plan regularly
It's important to review this plan periodically to ensure it remains
relevant. As you experience changes in your life, adjust the strategies
to fit what works best for you.

In this chapter, we've addressed preventing relapses in depression,
from identifying early warning signs to implementing coping
strategies and the importance of continuing preventive treatment.
The practical exercise has provided you with a personalized

approach to creating a relapse prevention plan to help maintain long-term emotional stability. Remember, the key to avoiding relapses is constant attention to your well-being, adapting your habits, and seeking support from others when needed.

Chapter 18: Stories of Overcoming Depression

Overcoming depression is not only a personal achievement but also a testament to the power of human resilience. Through the life stories of people who have faced this difficult battle, we can find inspiration and hope for those who are still struggling. In this chapter, we will hear real stories of overcoming depression, identify common factors that contributed to their success, offer words of encouragement for those still fighting, and conclude with a reflection on the incredible capacity for resilience that we all carry within us.

18.1. Real Stories of People Who Overcame Depression

Stories of overcoming remind us that while depression may seem like an endless struggle, many people have been able to move forward and regain their emotional well-being. Here, we present three real stories of individuals who faced depression and overcame it through perseverance, support, and appropriate treatment.

Story 1: María, 45 years old

María had always been an active and optimistic person, but after the sudden death of her mother, she began to feel a sadness that wouldn't go away. A lack of energy, insomnia, and loss of interest in everything she once loved took over her life. Initially, María thought she was simply going through the grieving process, but over time, her symptoms worsened. It became difficult for her to get out of bed, and she started distancing herself from friends and family.

With the support of her partner, María eventually decided to seek professional help. She attended therapy for a year, where she learned to process her grief and unresolved feelings she had suppressed for so long. She also started taking antidepressants under her doctor's supervision, which helped stabilize her mood while she worked on her emotional recovery. Now, María is an advocate for mental health, openly sharing her experience to help others.

Story 2: Raúl, 29 years old

Raúl was diagnosed with depression in college, but for years, he avoided talking about it due to shame and fear of stigma. Despite leading a seemingly successful life, with a good job and close friends, he felt empty and disconnected. Raúl tried to ignore his symptoms, convincing himself that he could handle it alone. However, he eventually reached a point where suicidal thoughts became constant, and after a crisis, he decided to see a therapist.

Cognitive-behavioral therapy (CBT) helped Raúl change his negative thought patterns, and he committed to regular exercise, which was crucial to improving his well-being. Little by little, with the support of his therapist and friends, Raúl began to feel more in control of his life and started enjoying the small things again. Today, he continues to attend therapy and has learned to proactively manage his mental health.

Story 3: Claudia, 63 years old

Claudia experienced depression after retirement, a time that, instead of being relaxing, made her feel lost and without purpose. After years of having a busy routine, the lack of daily structure and social isolation plunged her into a deep sadness. She stopped leaving the house and started suffering from sleep problems and anxiety.

A close friend eventually encouraged Claudia to speak with a psychologist who specialized in working with older adults. Through reminiscence therapy and participation in community activities, Claudia began to find new purpose in life. She joined a book club and started volunteering in her community. These small steps restored her sense of belonging and connection. Today, Claudia lives with a renewed sense of satisfaction and peace.

18.2. Common Factors in Success Stories

While each story of overcoming depression is unique, several common factors contributed to the success of those who managed to recover. These factors can serve as valuable guidance for those still fighting:

- **Seeking professional help:** In all cases, those who overcame depression sought help from psychologists, psychiatrists, or therapists. Therapy provided the space and tools necessary to work through emotions and heal.

- **Support from social networks:** Family and friends played a crucial role in recovery. Whether helping to recognize the problem or offering emotional support, close ones were a fundamental pillar in the process.

- **Commitment to treatment:** Whether through medication, therapy, or both, those who overcame depression committed to their treatment for the long term, even when results weren't immediate.

- **Lifestyle changes:** Incorporating changes in daily routines, such as exercise, healthy eating, and self-care, was key to improving mood and maintaining emotional stability.

- **Patience and perseverance:** Depression is a complex illness with no quick fix. All of these cases shared the trait of perseverance, as individuals understood that recovery takes time and that it's normal to experience ups and downs during the process.

18.3. Inspiration for Those Currently Struggling

If you are facing depression right now, the stories above may offer you hope. It's important to remember that you are not alone. Depression can make you feel isolated and without a way out, but many people have been in that same situation and have managed to overcome it.

Here are some words of encouragement for those still struggling:

- **Ask for help:** Taking the first step toward recovery, whether by talking to a friend or seeking a therapist, is crucial. Help is available, and seeking it is not a sign of weakness but of strength.

- **Don't give up:** Depression can be exhausting, and it may feel like things will never improve. However, with time and proper treatment, many people have found light at the end of the tunnel. Recovery is possible.

- **Take care of your body and mind:** Small changes in your routine, such as walking for a few minutes a day, improving your diet, or practicing deep breathing, can have a positive impact on your emotional state.

- **Lean on others:** Don't be afraid to rely on those around you. Talking about how you feel can lighten the burden, and emotional support is essential in tough times.

18.4. Reflection from the Doctor: Human Resilience

Resilience is the ability we all have to overcome adversity and emerge stronger. Depression can make you feel like your resilience has disappeared, but the truth is that it's still there, waiting to be activated. Throughout my career, I've seen people go through the darkest moments of their lives and find a way to recover.

Resilience doesn't mean you won't feel pain or sadness. It means that despite those feelings, you can find the strength to keep going. Sometimes, this strength comes from small steps: getting out of bed, taking a walk, talking to a friend, or going to therapy. Over time, those steps accumulate and build a path toward a more balanced and meaningful life.

It's important to remember that recovery isn't linear. There will be difficult days and better days, but what really matters is consistency. Just as a muscle strengthens with constant exercise, resilience grows as you continue to face challenges.

If you're reading this and you're in the middle of the fight, I want to remind you that although it may seem impossible now, recovery is real. And with the right treatment, the right support, and your own capacity for resilience, you can find your own way to overcome it.

This chapter has shared stories of people who have overcome depression, highlighting the common factors that contributed to their success and offering inspiration to those still struggling. The reflection on human resilience reminds us that we all have the ability to overcome adversity, even when it seems impossible. With patience, support, and treatment, recovery is possible, and these stories of triumph stand as proof of that.

Chapter 19: Final Reflection from the Doctor

Reaching the end of this book is only the beginning of a longer journey toward emotional well-being. Depression is a condition that affects millions of people worldwide, but it's important to remember that this is not a battle you need to fight alone. In this final chapter, I want to reflect on the importance of seeking help, the need to never give up, and how we should understand the path to recovery as an ongoing process. Finally, I will share a message of hope for all readers.

20.1. The Importance of Seeking Help

One of the most important lessons we can take from everything discussed in this book is that seeking help is crucial. Depression is a real illness, and like any other illness, it requires treatment. Just as you wouldn't hesitate to see a doctor if you had a physical ailment, you shouldn't hesitate to seek professional support when it comes to your mental health.

Many people suffering from depression feel that they must face it alone, either due to shame, fear of stigma, or the belief that asking for help is a sign of weakness. However, the opposite is true: asking for help is a sign of strength. Acknowledging that you need support and taking steps to get it is a fundamental step on the road to recovery.

Help can come in many forms: psychological therapy, medication, support groups, or simply sharing your feelings with a trusted friend or family member. No matter how you choose to receive support, what's important is that you know you are not alone and that there are resources and people willing to help you.

20.2. Why We Should Never Give Up

Depression can make us feel like there is no way out, that the pain is insurmountable, or that our lives can't improve. But as we have seen throughout this book, many people have been in that same dark place and found their way out. The key is to never give up.

It's normal that during the recovery process, there will be days when you feel better and others when everything seems to worsen again. These ups and downs are part of the process, and it's important to remember that, while setbacks may happen, they do not mean you are going backward entirely. Every day you choose to keep moving forward is a step toward healing.

Depression distorts our perception of reality and can make us feel like things will never get better. However, progress can be gradual, almost imperceptible at first. Not giving up means that even on the hardest days, you find a reason, no matter how small, to keep going. It might be a conversation with someone who cares about you, the satisfaction of overcoming an obstacle, or simply getting out of bed in the morning. Everything counts.

20.3. The Path to Recovery as a Continuous Journey

It's important to understand that recovering from depression is not a final destination but an ongoing journey. The idea that one day you will wake up and be "cured" is tempting, but the reality is that, like any aspect of health, mental health requires constant maintenance.

This doesn't mean that you will always live under the shadow of depression, but that it's possible to lead a full and balanced life by learning to recognize your emotional needs and taking care of them. The key is to always stay attuned to your well-being and proactively maintain healthy habits, both physically and mentally.

Recovery involves learning how to manage your emotions, developing effective coping strategies, and continuing to engage in activities and relationships that promote your well-being. There will be moments when you feel more vulnerable, and during those times, your tools and support network will be essential to keeping you on the right path.

It's also important to remember that self-care is not a luxury, but a necessity. Practicing self-compassion, allowing yourself to have difficult days without blaming yourself for them, is essential for sustainable recovery. Depression makes you believe that you are undeserving of care or love, but the truth is that you deserve all the attention and support you can receive, both from yourself and others.

20.4. Final Message to Readers

I want to conclude this book with a direct message to you, who have made it this far and may be struggling with your mental health, seeking answers, or simply trying to understand more about depression.

The first thing I want to tell you is that you are not alone. Depression makes you feel isolated, as though no one could understand what you are going through. But the reality is that many people have been through the same thing and have come out on the other side. There is always someone willing to listen and walk with you through this process.

The second thing I want you to remember is that depression does not define who you are. It is an illness, not a characteristic of your personality. You are not less valuable or capable because you suffer from depression. This dark moment doesn't have to define the rest of your life. There are many beautiful and rewarding things waiting for you if you keep moving forward, even when it seems impossible.

And finally, I want to encourage you to keep fighting. Every day that you choose not to give up is a victory. Every time you seek help, when you take care of yourself, when you express your emotions, you are taking control of your life. Depression can be a powerful force, but so are you. Within you is an incredible resilience that will allow you to overcome this challenge, just as millions of people before you have done.

The path to recovery can be long and sometimes difficult, but with support, patience, and a commitment to taking care of yourself, it's a path you can walk successfully. No matter how many times you stumble, what matters is that you get back up and keep moving forward. You deserve a full life, and recovery is possible.

Chapter 20: On the Side Effects of Antidepressants and Anxiolytics

Antidepressants and anxiolytics are crucial treatments for many people suffering from depression and anxiety disorders. While these medications can be highly effective in alleviating emotional and psychological symptoms, it's important to recognize that, like any pharmacological treatment, they can cause side effects that affect various parts of the body. In this chapter, we will explore the most common side effects of antidepressants and anxiolytics, how they can influence other areas of the body, and what to do if you experience these effects.

Side Effects of Antidepressants

Antidepressants are designed to regulate chemical imbalances in the brain, particularly neurotransmitters such as serotonin, dopamine, and norepinephrine, which are related to mood and emotions. The main types of antidepressants include selective serotonin reuptake inhibitors (SSRIs), serotonin-norepinephrine reuptake inhibitors (SNRIs), and tricyclic antidepressants. While these medications help improve mood and reduce depression symptoms, they can also cause side effects that affect other parts of the body.

Common Side Effects of Antidepressants:

- **Digestive issues:** Antidepressants, especially SSRIs, can cause stomach upset, nausea, vomiting, diarrhea, or constipation. This is because serotonin is present not only in the brain but also in the gastrointestinal tract, where it plays a role in regulating digestive movements.

- **Weight gain or loss:** Many antidepressants can affect appetite and metabolism. Some, like SSRIs, may decrease appetite initially, leading to weight loss, while others, like tricyclic antidepressants, may increase appetite and result in long-term weight gain.

- **Sexual dysfunction:** One of the most common side effects of antidepressants, particularly SSRIs and SNRIs, is sexual dysfunction. This can include decreased libido, difficulty achieving orgasm, or erectile dysfunction in men. This effect can impact quality of life, so it's important to discuss it with your doctor if it becomes a persistent issue.

- **Drowsiness or insomnia:** Some antidepressants, such as tricyclics, may cause drowsiness and fatigue, while others, like SSRIs, can lead to insomnia or sleep disturbances. This can make it difficult to get adequate rest, which in turn can exacerbate depression symptoms.

- **Dry mouth:** Tricyclic antidepressants and some SSRIs can cause dry mouth, increasing the risk of cavities and other dental problems if not managed properly.

- **Blurred vision:** Some antidepressants can affect visual focus and cause temporary blurred vision. This effect is more common at the beginning of treatment and usually improves over time.

- **Excessive sweating:** Some patients report increased sweating, especially at night. This may be due to changes in serotonin levels, which affect the body's temperature regulation.

Side Effects of Anxiolytics

Anxiolytics, such as benzodiazepines (diazepam, lorazepam, alprazolam) and SSRIs, are primarily used to treat anxiety but can also have side effects that affect other parts of the body. Benzodiazepines, in particular, act as sedatives and affect the central nervous system, which can lead to a range of unwanted effects.

Common Side Effects of Anxiolytics:

- **Sedation and drowsiness:** Benzodiazepines, which have a sedative effect, often cause excessive drowsiness and fatigue during the day. This can make it difficult to perform tasks that require attention and concentration, such as driving or working.

- **Memory problems:** Long-term use of benzodiazepines can affect short-term memory and the ability to retain information. This effect is particularly concerning in older adults, as it can increase the risk of developing cognitive problems over time.

- **Dependence and withdrawal:** Benzodiazepines are medications that can cause physical and psychological dependence if used long-term. If the medication is stopped suddenly, withdrawal symptoms can occur, such as anxiety, insomnia, tremors, or seizures.

- **Dizziness and balance issues:** People taking anxiolytics may experience dizziness, loss of balance, and falls, especially older adults. This is a particular risk for those with mobility issues or weakness.

- **Respiratory problems:** Benzodiazepines can depress the respiratory system, which can be dangerous for people with underlying respiratory issues, such as sleep apnea or chronic obstructive pulmonary disease (COPD).

- **Confusion and disorientation:** Some people, especially older adults, may experience confusion or feel disoriented when taking benzodiazepines. This effect can increase the risk of falls and accidents.

How to Manage Side Effects

If you experience side effects while taking antidepressants or anxiolytics, it's important to talk to your doctor or psychiatrist. You should never stop the medication on your own, as doing so abruptly can lead to withdrawal symptoms or worsen depression or anxiety. **Here are some tips for managing side effects:**

- **Consult your doctor about dosage adjustments:** Sometimes, side effects can be reduced by adjusting the medication dosage or changing the time of day you take it.

- **Explore alternatives:** There are different types of antidepressants and anxiolytics. If one medication is causing side effects that interfere with your quality of life, your doctor may suggest switching to another type of medication.

- **Lifestyle changes:** Regular exercise, a balanced diet, and practicing relaxation techniques (such as meditation or yoga) can help improve your overall well-being and reduce some side effects.

- **Psychological therapy:** In some cases, psychological therapies like Cognitive Behavioral Therapy (CBT) can be as effective as medications in treating depression and anxiety. Combining medication with therapy can help you rely less on medications in the long term.

Conclusion

While antidepressants and anxiolytics can be extremely helpful in treating the symptoms of depression and anxiety, it's important to be informed about the possible side effects that may affect other parts of the body. With proper supervision and open communication with your doctor, it's possible to manage these side effects and adjust the treatment to benefit you in the best way possible.

Chapter 21: Natural Remedies as Adjuncts in the Treatment of Depression and Anxiety

In addition to conventional treatments like antidepressants, anxiolytics, and psychological therapy, there is growing interest in the use of natural remedies as adjuncts in the treatment of depression and anxiety. While these remedies should not replace medical treatments, they can be helpful as a complement to improving overall well-being. In this chapter, we will explore some of the most common plants, supplements, and natural practices that have shown positive effects on mood and anxiety levels. We will also discuss their safety and how to integrate them alongside conventional treatments.

21.1. Medicinal Plants for Depression and Anxiety

Medicinal plants have been used for centuries in various cultures to treat mental health issues. Some have demonstrated beneficial effects as adjuncts in reducing symptoms of depression and anxiety. Below, we review some of the most studied plants:

1. St. John's Wort (Hypericum perforatum)

St. John's Wort is one of the most popular herbal remedies for mild to moderate depression. Studies suggest that this plant may be as effective as some commonly used antidepressants, as it acts on brain neurotransmitters like serotonin, dopamine, and norepinephrine.

Benefits:

- May improve mood and reduce symptoms of mild to moderate depression.

- Acts as a mild sedative, helping with sleep problems related to anxiety.

Precautions:

- St. John's Wort interacts with several medications, including contraceptives, antidepressants, blood thinners, and some cancer treatments. It is crucial to consult a doctor before taking it.

- It is not recommended for people already taking antidepressants, as it can cause serotonin syndrome, a dangerous condition caused by excessive levels of serotonin.

2. Valerian (Valeriana officinalis)

Valerian is a plant known for its sedative and relaxing properties, mainly used to treat insomnia and anxiety-related issues. By helping calm the nervous system, it can be useful for those suffering from anxiety or prolonged stress episodes.

Benefits:

- Improves sleep quality and relieves insomnia.

- Reduces muscle tension and promotes relaxation.

- **Precautions:**

- Valerian can cause daytime drowsiness if taken in excess. It's important to follow the recommended doses.

- It may interact with other sedatives, so it's necessary to consult a doctor if you are taking sleep or anxiety medications.

3. Ashwagandha (Withania somnifera)

Ashwagandha is an adaptogenic plant that has gained popularity in treating anxiety and depression. Adaptogens help the body manage stress and balance hormonal responses.

Benefits:

- Reduces cortisol levels (the stress hormone), which helps alleviate anxiety symptoms.

- Improves overall well-being and promotes balanced mood.
  Precautions:

- While generally safe, Ashwagandha may cause gastrointestinal discomfort in some individuals.

- It is not recommended during pregnancy or for those with thyroid issues without professional guidance.

4. Lavender (Lavandula angustifolia)

Lavender essential oil is known for its calming and relaxing properties. It is used both topically and in aromatherapy to relieve anxiety, stress, and improve sleep.

Benefits:

- Promotes relaxation and helps reduce anxiety.

- Improves sleep quality by reducing insomnia.

-

- **Precautions:**

- Although generally safe, some individuals may be sensitive to the essential oil and develop skin irritation. It should be properly diluted before topical application.

- Use with caution for individuals with respiratory conditions such as asthma.

21.2. Supplements for Depression and Anxiety

In addition to medicinal plants, certain supplements have also shown potential as support in treating depression and anxiety. Below, we review some of the most well-known supplements.

1. Omega-3 Fatty Acids

Omega-3 fatty acids, found in fatty fish (like salmon and sardines), are essential for brain health. Numerous studies have suggested that omega-3s may help reduce symptoms of depression and anxiety.

Benefits:

- Improves brain function and promotes neurotransmitter production.

- Reduces symptoms of mild to moderate depression.
  Precautions:

- Omega-3 supplements are generally safe, but in high doses, they may cause digestive issues or interact with blood thinners. It is best to take them under medical supervision.

2. Magnesium

Magnesium is an essential mineral that plays an important role in brain function and mood regulation. Magnesium deficiency has been linked to anxiety and depression.

Benefits:

- Helps reduce anxiety and improve mood.

- Promotes muscle relaxation and restful sleep.
Precautions:

- Magnesium is generally safe, but in high doses, it can cause diarrhea. It's important to follow recommended dosage instructions.

3. B Vitamins

B vitamins, especially B6, B9 (folic acid), and B12, are essential for producing neurotransmitters like serotonin and dopamine, which regulate mood.
Benefits:

- Helps combat fatigue and improves cognitive function.

- Contributes to reducing depressive symptoms.
Precautions:

- B vitamins are water-soluble, meaning excess amounts are excreted through urine. However, it's always recommended to consult a doctor before starting any supplement, especially if you are already taking other medications.

4. L-Theanine

L-theanine is an amino acid found in green tea that has been shown to have calming effects without causing drowsiness.
Benefits:

- Improves relaxation without sedation.

- Reduces anxiety and promotes mental clarity.
Precautions:

- It is generally considered safe but important to ensure it does not interact with other medications.

21.3. Complementary Practices for Mental Health

Along with natural remedies and supplements, certain practices can complement the treatment of depression and anxiety:

1. Meditation and Mindfulness

Meditation and mindfulness are practices that help people focus on the present moment and reduce rumination, one of the factors contributing to anxiety and depression.
Benefits:

- Reduces symptoms of stress and anxiety.

- Improves the ability to manage negative emotions and thoughts.

2. Yoga

Yoga combines conscious breathing, physical movement, and meditation. It has been shown to be effective in reducing cortisol levels and improving mood.
Benefits:

- Improves emotional balance and reduces stress.

- Promotes the connection between body and mind, helping manage anxiety.

3. Regular Physical Exercise

Exercise is one of the most effective ways to improve mood, as it promotes the release of endorphins, the "happy hormones."
Benefits:

- Improves physical and mental health.

- Reduces anxiety and improves sleep.

21.4. Precautions and Medical Consultation

While natural remedies can be helpful, it's crucial to remember that they should not replace conventional treatments without the guidance of a healthcare professional. Any supplement or medicinal plant should be taken under medical supervision, especially if you are taking prescription medications. The effects of natural remedies can vary from person to person, and some may interact with other pharmacological treatments, which can be potentially dangerous.

This chapter has explored natural remedies and complementary practices that can serve as adjuncts in the treatment of depression and anxiety. While these approaches can be helpful as support, it is essential to use them safely and in conjunction with conventional treatment. As always, the key lies in individualizing treatment, where each person must find the right balance between traditional medicine and natural remedies that best suit their needs.

Chapter 22: The Importance of Loved Ones for a Person with Depression and/or Anxiety

Depression and anxiety are disorders that not only affect those who suffer from them but also their family members, friends, and loved ones. In times of emotional suffering, people with depression or anxiety often feel isolated, misunderstood, and unable to ask for help. In this context, the support of loved ones can make a significant difference in the recovery process. In this chapter, we will explore the crucial role that loved ones play, how they can offer effective support, and how they can also take care of their own well-being while providing support.

22.1. The Importance of Emotional and Practical Support

People with depression or anxiety often feel overwhelmed by their emotions, which can lead them to withdraw, avoid social contact, or even isolate themselves completely. At these times, the intervention of loved ones is not only valuable but essential to help facilitate the path to recovery. The support of family and friends can act as an emotional anchor, reminding the person that they are not alone in their struggle.

Benefits of support from loved ones:

- **Reducing isolation:** Depression and anxiety often create feelings of loneliness and disconnection. A loved one can help break this cycle by providing companionship, understanding, and a safe space to express feelings.

- **Emotional validation:** Those struggling with these disorders often feel that their emotions are inappropriate or shameful.

Having someone who listens without judgment and validates what they are feeling can lighten that burden and provide comfort.

- **Encouraging professional help:** In many cases, people with depression or anxiety may resist seeking professional help due to stigma or fear. A loved one can act as a bridge, encouraging them to consult a therapist or doctor.

- **Practical help:** Daily tasks, such as grocery shopping, cooking, or household chores, can become overwhelming during an emotional crisis. Loved ones can offer practical assistance, allowing the person to focus on their recovery.

22.2. How Loved Ones Can Provide Effective Support

Supporting someone dealing with depression or anxiety is not always easy. However, there are several ways that loved ones can offer effective support without feeling powerless or overwhelmed by the situation.

Strategies for providing effective support:

- **Listen without judgment:** Often, people with depression or anxiety just need to be heard. Allowing space for them to express their emotions without offering immediate solutions can be very helpful. Phrases like "I'm listening," "I understand that this is hard for you," or "I'm here for whatever you need" are ways to show understanding.

- **Be patient:** Recovery from depression and anxiety takes time, and there will be good days and bad days. It's important not to pressure the person to "get better" quickly or to immediately overcome their problems. Patience is key, and it's essential for the person to feel they can move at their own pace.

- **Offer practical support:** Small actions can have a big impact. Offering to do the grocery shopping, accompany the person to a medical appointment, or help with daily tasks can relieve stress and allow the person to focus on their emotional well-being.

- **Avoid minimizing their feelings:** Often, people with good intentions try to cheer up their loved ones by saying things like "It's not that bad" or "Everything will be okay." While such phrases aim to ease the pain, they can make the person feel misunderstood or that their emotions are not taken seriously. Instead of minimizing their feelings, it's more helpful to say: "I know this is difficult, but I'll be here to support you."

- **Be present:** Sometimes, just being nearby can make a big difference. Accompanying the person without saying much, doing an activity together, or simply spending time in their company can provide a sense of security and comfort.

- **Encourage healthy habits:** Loved ones can help create a routine that promotes well-being, such as encouraging light exercise, healthy eating, or adequate rest. However, it's important to do this without imposing expectations or pressuring the person.

22.3. Avoiding Counterproductive Behaviors

Sometimes, unintentionally, loved ones may adopt behaviors that, while well-intentioned, can be counterproductive for the person suffering from depression or anxiety. It's important to be aware of these behaviors and avoid them to prevent worsening the situation.

Behaviors to avoid:

- **Pressuring to "overcome" depression or anxiety quickly:** Phrases like "You just need to think positively" or "Go out and have fun" can be harmful, as they imply that recovery depends solely on the person's willpower or attitude. Depression and anxiety are serious disorders and are not simply overcome by a change in mindset.

- **Minimizing the illness:** Depression and anxiety are real conditions, not just moods. Minimizing symptoms, such as saying "It's just a rough patch," can make the person feel misunderstood or alone in their pain.

- **Comparing to other experiences:** Avoid comparing the person's suffering with that of others or with personal experiences. Every situation is unique, and saying things like "I was depressed too, and I got over it" can devalue what the person is going through.

- **Taking control of the process:** While it's important to offer support, you should not take full control of the person's recovery process. It's essential to allow them to actively participate in their treatment and make decisions for themselves.

22.4. Taking Care of Your Own Well-Being While Offering Support

Helping a loved one with depression or anxiety can be emotionally exhausting. To provide the best possible support, caregivers must also take care of themselves. It's not selfish to attend to your own needs while caring for someone else; in fact, it's necessary to avoid emotional burnout.

Tips for loved ones:

- **Set boundaries:** Sometimes, it's necessary to set boundaries to protect your own well-being. This might mean defining moments of rest or recognizing when it's necessary to step back temporarily to recharge.

- **Seek your own support:** Loved ones may also need support. Talking to a friend, family member, or even a therapist can help process emotions and find strategies to manage the stress of caring for someone with depression or anxiety.

- **Accept what is beyond your control:** While you want to help, it's important to remember that you cannot "fix" someone else's depression or anxiety. Recovery is a process that depends on multiple factors, and your role is to provide support, not solve the problem.

- **Maintain balance in your personal life:** It's easy to dedicate all your emotional energy to helping a loved one, but it's essential to maintain a healthy balance in your own life. This includes dedicating time to your own interests, relationships, and well-being.

22.5. The Power of Love and Empathy

The support of loved ones can be a fundamental pillar in the recovery process from depression and anxiety. Love and empathy do not cure these disorders on their own, but they can provide the strength and courage needed for someone to seek help and continue fighting for their well-being. Knowing they are not alone and that someone is willing to walk beside them in their darkest moments can make all the difference.

In this chapter, we have explored how loved ones can significantly impact the life of a person with depression or anxiety. Whether providing emotional support, helping with daily tasks, or simply being present, the love and understanding of those around us are essential elements of recovery. At the same time, it's vital that caregivers also take care of themselves in order to offer consistent and effective support.

Appendices: Glossary of Terms Related to Depression

This glossary provides clear and simple definitions of key terms related to depression. It is useful for gaining a better understanding of the common concepts and terms that arise in the treatment and diagnosis of depression and associated disorders.

- **Adaptogens**: Natural substances, usually derived from plants, that help the body adapt to stress and balance its functions. Examples include ashwagandha and ginseng.

- **Anhedonia**: Loss of interest or pleasure in activities that were previously rewarding or enjoyable. It is one of the main symptoms of depression.

- **Anxiety**: A feeling of excessive worry, nervousness, or unease. It can occur alongside depression and may be chronic in anxiety disorders.

- **Antidepressants**: Medications used to treat symptoms of depression. The most common types include SSRIs (Selective Serotonin Reuptake Inhibitors), SNRIs (Serotonin and Norepinephrine Reuptake Inhibitors), and tricyclic antidepressants.

- **Benzodiazepines**: A group of sedative medications used to treat anxiety and sleep disorders. They can cause dependency if used long-term.

- **Cortisol**: A hormone released by the body in response to stress. Chronically elevated cortisol levels can be linked to depression and anxiety.

- **Panic Attack**: Sudden episodes of intense fear accompanied by physical symptoms such as heart palpitations, sweating, and shortness of breath. Common in anxiety disorders.

- **Major Depression**: A form of depression characterized by persistent feelings of sadness, hopelessness, and loss of interest in most activities for at least two consecutive weeks.

- **Postpartum Depression**: A type of depression that affects women after childbirth. It is characterized by deep sadness, fatigue, irritability, and difficulties caring for the newborn.

- **Dysthymia (Persistent Depressive Disorder)**: A chronic form of long-lasting depression, with less severe symptoms than major depression but that can persist for years.

- **Antidepressant-induced Sexual Dysfunction**: A common side effect of some antidepressants, especially SSRIs, which may include loss of sexual desire, difficulty reaching orgasm, or erectile dysfunction.

- **Post-Traumatic Stress Disorder (PTSD)**: An anxiety disorder that develops after experiencing a traumatic event. It can cause flashbacks, intense anxiety, and avoidance of situations that remind the individual of the trauma.

- **Chronic Fatigue**: A constant feeling of tiredness and lack of energy, which may be related to depression or other physical conditions.

- **St. John's Wort**: An herbal remedy used to treat mild to moderate depression. However, it can interact with many medications and should be taken with caution.

- **Selective Serotonin Reuptake Inhibitors (SSRIs)**: A common type of antidepressant that works by increasing serotonin levels in the brain. Examples include fluoxetine, sertraline, and escitalopram.

- **Serotonin and Norepinephrine Reuptake Inhibitors (SNRIs)**: Antidepressants that increase both serotonin and norepinephrine in the brain. Examples include venlafaxine and duloxetine.

- **Mindfulness**: A practice of focused attention that involves concentrating on the present and accepting thoughts and emotions without judgment. It is useful in managing stress, anxiety, and depression.

- **Neurotransmitters**: Chemicals in the brain that transmit signals between neurons. Imbalances in neurotransmitters such as serotonin, dopamine, and norepinephrine are linked to depression.

- **Psychotherapy**: Psychological treatment for mental disorders that involves talking with a therapist. Cognitive Behavioral Therapy (CBT) is one of the most commonly used forms for treating depression.

- **Relapse**: The return of depressive symptoms after a period of improvement. It is common in individuals with chronic or recurrent depression.

- **Resilience**: The ability to recover from difficult or traumatic situations. In the context of depression, it refers to the ability to cope with and overcome depressive episodes.

- **Serotonin Syndrome**: A potentially dangerous reaction that can occur when medications increase serotonin levels in the brain too much. Symptoms include confusion, fever, agitation, and in severe cases, it can be life-threatening.

- **Somatization**: The process by which emotions or psychological issues manifest as physical symptoms, such as headaches, digestive problems, or bodily pain, without an evident physical cause.

- **Suicide**: The intentional act of taking one's own life. Depression is a major risk factor, and individuals with suicidal thoughts should seek professional help immediately.

- **Cognitive Behavioral Therapy (CBT)**: A form of psychotherapy that focuses on changing negative thought patterns and problematic behaviors. It is one of the most effective treatments for depression and anxiety.

- **Acceptance and Commitment Therapy (ACT)**: A type of psychotherapy that teaches people to accept their difficult emotions and thoughts rather than fight them, and to commit to actions aligned with their personal values.

- **Generalized Anxiety Disorder (GAD)**: A disorder characterized by excessive and persistent worry about various everyday life situations. It often coexists with depression.

- **Seasonal Affective Disorder (SAD)**: A type of depression that occurs at certain times of the year, usually in the winter months, when there is less sunlight. It is believed to be related to changes in serotonin and melatonin levels in the brain.

- **Bipolar Disorder**: A mental disorder characterized by extreme mood swings, including episodes of depression and episodes of mania or hypomania (elevated mood).

Tricyclic Antidepressants: An older class of antidepressants used to treat depression. While effective, they tend to have more side effects than more modern antidepressants.

- **Valerian**: A plant used in herbal medicine for its sedative and relaxing properties, primarily to treat anxiety and insomnia.

Depression Diagnosis

Table 1: Difference Between Sadness and Clinical Depression

Characteristics	Sadness	Clinical Depression
Duration	Temporary, lasting days/weeks	Persistent, lasting at least 2 weeks
Clear cause	Related to a specific event	May not have a clear cause
Impact on daily life	Does not significantly interfere	Severely affects daily activities
Physical symptoms	Generally absent	Fatigue, insomnia, changes in appetite
Suicidal thoughts	Rare	Possible in severe cases

Table 2: Common Diagnostic Tools for Depression

Tool	Description
PHQ-9 Questionnaire	A 9-question evaluation to measure the severity of depression
Hamilton Depression Scale (HAM-D)	A clinical interview to assess depression severity

Beck Depression Inventory (BDI)	A self-assessment questionnaire to measure depressive symptoms

Table 3: Common Side Effects of Antidepressants

Type of Antidepressant	Most Common Side Effects
SSRIs	Nausea, insomnia, sexual dysfunction
SNRIs	Sweating, fatigue, increased blood pressure
Tricyclic Antidepressants	Dry mouth, drowsiness, weight gain, constipation

Table 4: Types of Exercise Recommended for Depression

Type of Exercise	Mental Health Benefits
Aerobic exercise (running, swimming)	Increases endorphin and serotonin levels, improves sleep
Yoga and meditation	Reduces stress and promotes mental relaxation
Strength training	Improves self-esteem, boosts energy, reduces fatigue

Table 5: Strategies to Prevent Relapse in Depression

Strategy	Description
Continue therapy	Regular sessions to monitor progress and challenges
Regular self-care	Establish habits of healthy eating, exercise, and rest
Social support network	Maintain positive relationships with friends, family, or support groups
Recognize early signs	Identify early symptoms and act promptly

Table 6: Medicinal Plants for Depression and Anxiety

Medicinal Plant	Properties	Precautions
St. John's Wort	Improves mood in mild to moderate cases	Interacts with many medications
Valerian	Promotes relaxation, improves sleep	May cause daytime drowsiness
Ashwagandha	Reduces stress, improves resilience	Avoid in individuals with thyroid issues
Lavender	Calming effects, reduces anxiety	Possible skin irritation if applied topically

This glossary serves as a helpful guide for understanding key terms related to depression and anxiety, facilitating the comprehension of disorders and associated treatments.

Resources and Recommended Readings

Below is a selection of resources and recommended readings on depression, anxiety, and mental health in general. These books, websites, and organizations can provide additional information, support, and useful tools for those dealing with mental health issues, as well as for their loved ones.

1. Recommended Books on Depression and Anxiety

1.1. *The Noonday Demon: An Atlas of Depression* – Andrew Solomon

This book offers a deep exploration of depression, drawing from the author's personal experience as well as clinical and cultural perspectives. It combines science, history, and personal narratives to explain the profound impact depression has on people's lives.

1.2. *The Happiness Trap* – Russ Harris

Based on Acceptance and Commitment Therapy (ACT), this book helps readers free themselves from the constant pursuit of happiness and embrace difficult emotions, teaching strategies to create a more fulfilling and meaningful life.

1.3. *Mindfulness: An Eight-Week Plan for Finding Peace in a Frantic World* – Mark Williams and Danny Penman

This book introduces readers to mindfulness practice as an effective tool for managing anxiety and depression. It includes practical exercises and an evidence-based approach.

1.4. *Feeling Good: The New Mood Therapy* – David D. Burns

A classic in Cognitive Behavioral Therapy (CBT), this book provides tools to help readers change negative thinking patterns that contribute to depression and anxiety through practical exercises.

1.5. *Mental Health for Everyone* – **Laura Rojas-Marcos**

In this accessible and straightforward book, psychologist Laura Rojas-Marcos emphasizes the importance of taking care of our mental health, offering practical strategies and advice for improving emotional well-being.

2. Websites and Online Resources

2.1. Fundación ANAED (Asociación Nacional de Ayuda al Enfermo de Depresión)

www.anaed.org

A nonprofit organization that offers support to people with depression and their families. It provides information, advice, and resources for the treatment and understanding of depression.

2.2. Federación Española de Asociaciones de Ayuda al Trastorno Depresivo (FEAFES)

www.feafes.org

FEAFES unites associations that work to support people with depressive disorders and their families in Spain. They offer support programs, resources, and activities to raise awareness about depression.

2.3. Asociación Española de Psiquiatría Privada (ASEPP)

www.asepp.org

This site provides information on mental health, with a focus on depression and anxiety. It offers resources on treatments, medications, and psychiatric professionals.

2.4. Mental Health America (in English)

www.mhanational.org

A nonprofit organization that offers a wide range of resources, information, and support on mental health, including free assessment tools and self-help resources.

2.5. Headspace (in English)

A platform offering meditation and mindfulness programs to combat anxiety, stress, and depression. It also has a user-friendly app with guided exercises and relaxation courses.

2.6. National Institute of Mental Health (NIMH) (in English)

A reliable resource with research, articles, and guides on mental health disorders, including depression and anxiety. It offers updated information based on scientific studies.

3. Useful Mobile Apps

3.1. Calm

One of the most popular meditation and mindfulness apps, Calm offers programs and exercises to improve sleep, reduce stress, and manage anxiety. It includes guided sessions and relaxing music.

3.2. Headspace

Another excellent meditation app, Headspace specializes in mindfulness and relaxation exercises. It's designed to improve general well-being and help those struggling with anxiety and depression.

3.3. Sanvello (formerly Pacifica)

This app focuses on emotional well-being and managing anxiety and depression. It combines Cognitive Behavioral Therapy tools with meditation techniques and mood tracking.

3.4. Moodpath

An app that offers mood tracking to detect symptoms of depression and anxiety. It includes an emotional journal and exercise suggestions based on Cognitive Behavioral Therapy.

4. Organizations and Support Lines

4.1. Teléfono de la Esperanza

www.telefonodelaesperanza.org
A free helpline in Spain offering emotional support to people going through crises. Phone: 717 003 717.

4.2. Asociación Española Contra el Cáncer – Psychological Support

www.aecc.es
They offer psychological support for people suffering from depression or anxiety as a result of a cancer diagnosis. They also have specific programs for family members and patients.

4.3. Mind (in English)

www.mind.org.uk
A UK-based organization that provides support and resources for people with mental health issues. They offer helplines and an extensive database of articles on emotional well-being.

4.4. Samaritans (in English)

www.samaritans.org
A UK charity providing emotional support and helplines 24/7 for people experiencing suicidal thoughts or severe emotional crises.

5. Recommended Documentaries and Talks

5.1. *Depression: Out of the Shadows*

This PBS documentary explores depression from the perspective of those who have experienced it and mental health professionals. It examines the science behind depression, its treatments, and the impact it has on people's lives.

5.2. *The Mind Explained* (Netflix)

This documentary series offers a clear and accessible view of various aspects of mental health, including anxiety, depression, and meditation, explaining the science behind these disorders and their treatment.

5.3. TED Talk: *The Power of Vulnerability* – Brené Brown

In this talk, Brené Brown explores the power of vulnerability, emotional connection, and the need to accept difficult emotions as part of the healing process.

5.4. TED Talk: *Depression, the Secret We Share* – Andrew Solomon

Writer Andrew Solomon reflects on his own experience with depression in a moving talk that explores how it affects people and what is needed to overcome it.

This list of resources and recommended readings provides a helpful guide for deepening knowledge of depression, anxiety, and mental health. Whether through books, websites, apps, or documentaries, these materials can offer support, tools, and hope for those suffering from these disorders and their loved ones, helping them on the road to recovery.

Webography

Below is a list of reliable sources and websites used to compile and verify the information provided in the chapters and related graphics on depression, anxiety, and their treatments. These resources offer up-to-date scientific data, clinical research, and support on mental health topics.

1. **MedlinePlus**
   - URL: https://medlineplus.gov
   - Description: MedlinePlus is a resource from the U.S. National Library of Medicine that provides reliable medical information on a wide range of diseases, including mental disorders such as depression and anxiety. It was used for information on treatments, medication side effects, and self-care strategies.

2. **National Institute of Mental Health (NIMH)**
   - URL: https://www.nimh.nih.gov
   - Description: NIMH is a leading source of scientific information on mental disorders. The NIMH website was instrumental in obtaining clinical data on depression, its treatment, and the most effective therapies.

3. **Mayo Clinic**
   - URL: https://www.mayoclinic.org
   - Description: Mayo Clinic is one of the world's leading medical organizations. It offers evidence-based information on the symptoms, diagnoses, and treatments of depression and anxiety. It was used to gather information on various therapies, natural treatments, and symptoms of relapse.

4. **World Health Organization (WHO)**
   - URL: https://www.who.int
   - Description: The World Health Organization provides global data on the prevalence of depression, its social impact,

and strategies for its treatment. It was helpful in obtaining
information on risk factors, long-term treatment, and the
importance of social support.

5. **World Federation for Mental Health (WFMH)**
   • URL: https://wfmh.global
   • Description: This organization is dedicated to promoting
   mental health worldwide. It offers resources and educational
   campaigns to raise awareness about mental disorders,
   including depression and anxiety.

6. **American Psychological Association (APA)**
   • URL: https://www.apa.org
   • Description: The APA is an authority on psychology and
   mental health. Information on various psychological
   therapies, such as Cognitive Behavioral Therapy (CBT) and
   Acceptance and Commitment Therapy (ACT), was sourced
   from its publications and resources.

7. **National Institute for Health and Care Excellence (NICE)**
   • URL: https://www.nice.org.uk
   • Description: NICE is a UK-based organization that provides
   evidence-based clinical guidelines. Its guidance on managing
   depression and anxiety was essential for gathering
   information on best clinical practices and recommended
   treatments.

8. **Spanish Foundation of Psychiatry and Mental Health
   (FEPSM)**
   • URL: https://www.fepsm.org
   • Description: FEPSM offers information and resources on
   mental disorders in Spain. It was useful for obtaining local
   and up-to-date information on the treatment of depression and
   anxiety.

9. **Spanish Federation of Associations Supporting
    Depressive Disorders (FEAFES)**
    • URL: https://www.feafes.org
    • Description: FEAFES is a network of associations in Spain
    that provides support to individuals with depressive disorders
    and their families. Its resources were key to understanding the
    social and emotional support in depression treatment.

10. **The Mental Health Foundation**
    • URL: https://www.mentalhealth.org.uk
    • Description: A UK-based organization providing resources
    on mental health, prevention, and recovery. Its site was a
    significant source for relapse prevention strategies and
    caregiver support resources.

These sources have been selected for their reliability, scientific focus, and accessibility. The information has been reviewed and used to ensure that the book's content is based on current and well-founded data on depression, anxiety, and their treatments.